SONGS
of a
SUFFERING
KING

ALSO BY J. V. FESKO

SONGS
of a
SUFFERING
KING

The Grand Christ Hymn of Psalms 1–8

J. V. Fesko

Reformation Heritage Books
Grand Rapids, MI

Reformation Heritage Books
2965 Leonard St. NE
Grand Rapids, MI 49525
616-977-0889
e-mail: orders@heritagebooks.org
website: www.heritagebooks.org

Printed in the United States of America
20 21 22 23 24 25/10 9 8 7 6 5 4 3 2

Fesko, J. V., 1970-
  Songs of a suffering king : the grand Christ hymn of Psalms 1-8 / J.V. Fesko.
     pages cm
  ISBN 978-1-60178-310-3 (pbk. : alk. paper) 1. Bible. Psalms I-VIII—Devotional literature. I. Title.
  BS1430.54.F47 2014
  223'.206—dc23
                              2013050597

For additional Reformed literature, request a free book list from Reformation Heritage Books at the above regular or email address.

To
Bryan Estelle

Contents

Preface

I believe that the book of Psalms is vitally needed for the life and spiritual well-being of the church. Sadly, the Psalms no longer have a place of prominence in the worship of the broader church or even within many Reformed churches. Perhaps part of the reason for this dearth of the Psalms is the church's unfamiliarity with this wonderful, divinely inspired hymnbook. I hope this little book helps to awaken the church to the majesty, beauty, and splendor of the book of Psalms. May people long to read and discover Christ in the Psalms so that they follow in the footsteps of the disciples on the road to Emmaus when Jesus taught them all the things concerning His ministry written in "the Law of Moses and the Prophets and the Psalms" (Luke 24:44). Scriptural psalms should be a regular staple in our personal spiritual diet, whether we read, pray, or sing them in public or private worship. To that end I have included metrical versions of Psalms 1–8 from several different sources and have listed a suitable tune that can be accessed on the Internet to go along with each one.

I am grateful for a number of people who played a role in helping me complete this book: Jay Collier at Reformation Heritage Books, who approached me about the possibility of writing another book for them; Joel Beeke and the RHB staff for their willingness and all their work to publish the book; and my wife and three children (Val, Rob, and Carmen), not only for their sacrifice so that I have time to work on writing projects but also for their love and support. Thank you, Anneke, for your love and encouragement to write this book! It was your wonderful idea. I just hope that what I have written meets the mark, edifies the church, and brings glory to Christ our Savior.

I dedicate this book to my colleague and good friend Bryan Estelle, professor of Old Testament at Westminster Seminary California and minister in the Orthodox Presbyterian Church. Bryan is a good colleague and careful scholar, but in his heart of hearts he is a churchman through and through. And like most good churchmen, he does not trumpet his service, so people know little of his sacrifice for and service to Christ's church. Bryan spent the last few years working on the Psalter-Hymnal Committee for our denomination, the Orthodox Presbyterian Church. He has dutifully served on this committee by translating the entire Psalter so the members would have access to the treasures of the Scriptures in the original Hebrew. My prayer is that Bryan's labors, along with those of the rest of the committee, would return a tremendous and bountiful harvest in the worship and piety of Christians for generations to come.

—J. V. Fesko
Escondido, California

Introduction

Andrew Fletcher, an eighteenth-century Scottish writer, once observed that if a person were permitted to write the songs of a nation, he had no concern about who might create its laws.[1] Fletcher's idea was that music has great power to shape the life, practice, and ethos of a people. Songs have been written to rally nations to war, comfort people in the midst of great sorrow and despair, and cheer and gladden the heart in times of celebration. For example, if you watch the Olympics, you have probably seen Olympic athletes perched atop the medal stand who are overcome with emotion when their national anthem plays. Some readers may recall how music from the 1960s rallied and steeled the resolve of many young people in the United States against the Vietnam War. Songs like Creedence Clearwater Revival's "Fortunate Son" come to mind. How many times have you been riding in the car and heard an old song on the radio that brought back a flood of memories, perhaps of a specific place, time, or people? I can remember hearing Aaron Copland's "Fanfare

1. Andrew Fletcher, *An Account of a Conversation Concerning the Right Regulation of Governments for the Common Good of Mankind* (Edinburgh, 1703), 10.

for the Common Man" for the first time and feeling a
lump form in my throat because the music gripped me in
a powerful way.

Music is powerful, and it can be misused. However,
in the hands of our faithful covenant Lord, it has been
rightly embedded in the life of the covenant community,
the church, through the Bible's songbook, the Psalms.
The book of Psalms, also called the Psalter, is the biggest
book in the Bible, but for many in the church its contents
are largely mysterious and out of sight. Many people in
the church are familiar with certain psalms such as Psalm
23 or perhaps Psalms 2 and 110. Some people might drift
toward the end of the Psalter when they are in search
of words of praise or thanksgiving in times of prayer or
scriptural meditation. Two important characteristics about
the Psalter, however, might not immediately register in
the minds of some of its readers.

First, the *entire* Psalter is connected to the person and
work of Christ. One statement I have frequently heard
is that there are certain christological psalms—in other
words, psalms that explicitly reveal Christ, such as Psalm 2,
in which the Lord's Anointed, the Messiah, is enthroned.
But when Jesus was walking on the road to Emmaus with
His two disciples, He told them: "These are the words
which I spoke to you while I was still with you, that all
things must be fulfilled which were written in the Law of
Moses and the Prophets and the Psalms concerning Me"
(Luke 24:44). A quick perusal of the number of times different psalms appear in the New Testament through direct
quotation, echo, or allusion indicates that Jesus did not

have just a few isolated psalms in mind.[2] This does not mean that Christ explicitly appears, as He does in Psalm 2, in every psalm. Rather, a particular psalm might have the Messiah as a subject; it could describe aspects of His work such as intercession, or it might provide a prophetic window into His sufferings.

One of the things that readers of the Psalter should realize is that even though King David, the principal author of the Psalter, writes of his own sorrows, troubles, victories, and praises, he is a type, or foreshadow, of his Greater Son, Jesus, who is the antitype, or fulfillment. What the Psalms say of David as a messiah (remember, *messiah* means "anointed," and he was Israel's anointed king) is prophetic of Jesus as *the* Messiah. Dietrich Bonhoeffer observed this connection between David and Jesus:

> According to the witness of the Bible, David, as the anointed king of the chosen people of God, is a prototype of Jesus Christ. What befalls David occurs for the sake of the one who is in him and who is to proceed from him, namely Jesus Christ. David did not remain unaware of this, but "being therefore a prophet, and knowing that God had sworn with an oath to him that he would set one of his descendants upon his throne, he foresaw and spoke of the resurrection of the Christ" [Acts 2:30].

Bonhoeffer remarks that David prefigured Christ in his kingly office, his life, and his words. And even the

---

2. See, for example, the thirty-two columns of references to the Psalter in the index of *Commentary on the New Testament Use of the Old Testament*, ed. G. K. Beale and D. A. Carson (Grand Rapids: Baker Academic, 2007), 1176–82.

words that David prayed were ultimately Christ's. Hence, "this short observation about the New Testament sheds significant light on the entire Psalter. It refers the Psalter to Christ."[3]

Second, I suspect that most Psalter readers assume that the book is randomly arranged, like a potpourri or grab bag of theological observations. But there is a specific organizational structure to the whole Psalter that is most readily observable in its fivefold division. In fact, according to ancient rabbinic tradition, Moses gave Israel the five books of the Pentateuch (Genesis, Exodus, Leviticus, Numbers, and Deuteronomy), and David gave the nation the five books of the Psalter (Book 1: Psalms 1–41; Book 2: Psalms 42–72; Book 3: Psalms 73–89; Book 4: Psalms 90–106; Book 5: Psalms 107–150).[4] Many have noted that Psalm 1 serves as the broad introduction to the whole book, as the psalmist reflects upon the righteous man who delights in the "law of the LORD" (v. 2), which, in this context, refers not to the Decalogue but to the Lord's teaching in general—that is, what we find in the rest of the 149 psalms. In the subsequent books of the Psalter, each section ends with doxology and praise, and there are royal psalms at the seams of the first three books, such as Psalms 2, 72, and 89.[5]

---

3. Dietrich Bonhoeffer, *The Prayerbook of the Bible*, in *Dietrich Bonhoeffer Works*, ed. Gerhard Ludwig Miller and Albrecht Schonherr (Minneapolis: Fortress, 1996), 5:158–59.

4. Gerald Henry Wilson, *The Editing of the Hebrew Psalter* (Chico, Calif.: Scholars Press, 1985), 199–200.

5. Wilson, *Hebrew Psalter*, 208.

We can observe some of the deliberate editorial arrange-
ment of the Psalter when we consider the "bookends" of
Book 1, which begins with Psalm 2 (assuming that Psalm
1 is the introduction to the entire Psalter) and ends with
Psalm 41. Psalm 2 introduces the Davidic covenant, even
though it is not specifically mentioned (cf. 2 Sam. 7:14). In
Psalm 2 David writes:

"I will declare the decree:
The LORD has said to Me,
'You are My Son,
Today I have begotten You.
Ask of Me, and I will give You
The nations for Your inheritance,
And the ends of the earth for Your possession.
You shall break them with a rod of iron;
You shall dash them to pieces like a potter's
    vessel.'" (vv. 7–9)

God promises the Davidic scion that despite the scheming
of the kings of the earth (vv. 2–3), He will ensure that His
throne remains secure, a theme that resurfaces in Psalm 41:

Blessed is he who considers the poor;
The LORD will deliver him in time of trouble.
The LORD will preserve him and keep him alive,
And he will be blessed on the earth;
You will not deliver him to the will of his enemies….

By this I know that You are well pleased with me,
Because my enemy does not triumph over me.
As for me, You uphold me in my integrity,

And set me before Your face forever.
   (vv. 1–2, 11–12)[6]

The deliberate ordering of the psalms has important implications for how we read the book.

Rather than reading each psalm as an independent set of observations, we should instead view each as comprising a chapter in one grand story. Think of the chapters of the Psalter like the songs on a music album. Musicians have resisted the move from albums (CDs, cassettes, and vinyl LPs for those of us who are a bit older) to the iTunes world because they arranged the songs on their albums in a specific way to tell a story. But in the iTunes generation, a person can pick and choose the songs he wants—he can buy one song or several, but in the end the consumer "ruins" the final artistic product. Whether iTunes has ruined music albums is beside the point, but the analogy bears upon our reading and use of the Psalter. Seldom do readers recognize that the book of Psalms is telling a story, with each subsequent psalm serving a distinct function and purpose within the broader narrative. The challenge in observing the narrative pattern over the course of the whole Psalter can be daunting in this large book. However, we can peer into the beautiful literary structure and ordering of the Psalter through the examination of one small portion of it. In this case, we will examine Psalms 1–8.

I suspect that many people are familiar with Psalms 1, 2, and 8 because they appear at the beginning of the Psalter and deal with familiar themes. Most of us open a book and start by reading the first chapter. And in the case of

---

6. Wilson, *Hebrew Psalter*, 209–10.

themes such as the Messiah or the creation of man, Psalms 2 and 8 feature prominently. However, what about Psalms 3–7? For many Christians, these psalms probably represent uncharted territory. But if we keep in mind the intentional ordering of the Psalter, then the ground between Psalms 2 and 8 creates new questions. The whole Psalter is about Christ, so Psalm 1 speaks of the righteous man, ultimately Christ, who is blessed by God; Psalm 2 then segues to the enthronement of that righteous man, the Messiah. Psalm 8 initially appears to be about the creation of the first Adam, but in the hands of New Testament authors it is authoritatively applied to the last Adam, Jesus Christ (cf. Ps. 8; 1 Cor. 15:20–28). But what about the intervening passages? How can Psalm 2 end on a mountaintop with the enthronement of the Messiah and then descend into the valley of despair with the psalmist crying out to the Lord for deliverance from his enemies in Psalms 3–7?

Some might think that royal identity and suffering are mutually exclusive categories; the apostle Peter was of this mind-set when he rebuked Christ for what he perceived to be "negative talk" of suffering and crucifixion—ideas that the apostle initially believed were antithetical to his concept of a victorious Messiah. Peter, of course, merited Christ's quick and stinging rebuke (Matt. 16:22–28). Royal identity as the King of kings and suffering are not mutually exclusive categories, as the life of Christ manifestly demonstrates. Jesus was both the long-ago prophesied Davidic heir to the throne of Israel and the Suffering Servant of Isaiah in chapters 40–55. The motif of the suffering king unquestionably plays out in David's life on numerous occasions. The prophet Samuel anointed

David as king only for Saul to persecute and try to kill him (1 Sam. 16–31). We can only imagine David's descent into utter despair from the exhilaration of being anointed king. Such a pattern fits the unfolding narrative of Psalms 2–7, which then ends on a high note of praise and exaltation. In other words, we see that David prefigures Jesus in his mountaintop experience that ends in despair when Christ's glorious birth, attended by the angelic host and accompanied by gifts of royalty, quickly descends into fleeing from persecution and those who sought to kill Him, which continues in His ministry and culminates in His death. But Christ's death was not the final word; rather, Christ's exaltation through His resurrection and royal inauguration was the penultimate step in the completion of His work, only to be followed by His second coming.

When we become aware of this unfolding narrative pattern in the Psalter as a whole and Psalms 1–8 more narrowly, we read the Psalms in the light of Christ, which opens a new vista upon David's cries of dereliction. David's cries become those of Christ. Though the passage lies beyond the scope of this modest book, Christ's cry of dereliction upon the cross—"My God, My God, why have You forsaken me?"—confirms the David-Jesus connection (Ps. 22:1). So often the Gospels record Christ in times of prayer, but we never know the specific content of His prayers. And while we ultimately cannot know the specific content of Christ's prayers, except for what is recorded in the Gospels, the book of Psalms can give us an idea of the types of things that Christ might have prayed. It can provide a divinely inspired window into the heart of Christ. Ultimately, the Psalter as a whole trumpets the person and work of Christ, and we can examine a small slice of the Psalter's grand Christ hymn in Psalms 1–8.

What follows in each of the subsequent chapters is a devotional exploration of the first eight psalms. Each chapter explores the psalm in its original context. In other words, what was occurring in the life of David to occasion the psalm? After establishing the original historical context, we can consider the connections to Christ. In what way does the psalm speak of Christ? Last, after establishing the connections to Christ, we then consider the connections to the church, those who are united to Christ. In other words, when we read of the blessed man of Psalm 1, our thoughts should drift to how we might flee wickedness and render our obedience to God only after we have considered him in historical context and how he is connected to Christ.

Whatever obedience we might offer, even as regenerate Christians, is always tainted and stained with sin. As the Heidelberg Catechism asks, "But why cannot our good works be the whole or part of our righteousness before God?" It then answers: "The righteousness which can stand before the tribunal of God must be absolutely perfect and wholly conformable to the divine law, while even our best works in this life are all imperfect and defiled with sin" (Q. 62). Rather, if we recognize that David has one person in mind—namely, the man Jesus— then the gates of paradise are opened. Christ is the One who has not walked in the counsel of the wicked or stood in the way of sinners or sat in the seat of scoffers. The Lord has recognized Christ's righteousness, or obedience, and has blessed Him. When we ask how we can apply

Psalm 1, if we first focus upon Christ as the righteous man, we can then acknowledge that anyone united to Him receives the blessings He has secured. Only then, in Christ as branches united to the one true vine, can we meditate upon the law of God and delight in it and yield the fruit of righteousness in its season.

In addition to each exposition, I have included a series of questions to spark further reflection and study, whether privately or with a small group such as a Sunday school class or Bible study. But I would be remiss if I did not encourage readers not only to study the Psalter but also to sing it. Granted, the Psalter has been called the prayer book of the Bible and has assisted countless Christians in their prayers, whether in times of joy or sorrow, plenty or want. But as sixteenth-century Protestant Reformer John Calvin once observed, biblical worship songs are simply prayers in song form. What better way, then, to cement the truths of the psalm you have just studied than to use it in prayer and private and public worship? To facilitate the singing of these psalms, each chapter concludes with a metrical version of it. If you do not know how to play the piano, you can find a number of resources available on the Internet that include digital files of the tunes for each psalm so you can sing the psalm either alone or with a group. You need not choose between writing a nation's songs or laws. Instead, you can sing the law of God (His teaching) as it has been revealed in the Psalter. The old saying from Augustine remains relevant to us: "*Tolle et lege*" (Take up and read)! To this we can add, "*Tolle et cantare*" (Take up and sing)!

▶ Resources for Psalm Singing

Internet

www.psalter.org

> This website has a terrific library of MP3 files and includes tunes associated with the *Trinity Psalter*, *The Book of Psalms for Worship*, and *The Book of Psalms for Singing*.

www.psalter.com

> This website is devoted exclusively to *The Book of Psalms for Singing* and has the entire Psalter along with digital MP3 files.

Psalters

Trinity Psalter: Psalms 1–150 Words-Only Edition, ed. Terry Johnson (Pittsburgh: Crown & Covenant Publications, 1994).

> This is a great resource and has one version of each of the 150 psalms. This edition is words only, but you can find the tunes either online or in other hymnals or you can purchase the piano-player's edition, which has the music: *Trinity Psalter: Music Edition* (Pittsburgh: Crown & Covenant Publications, 2000).

The Book of Psalms for Singing (Pittsburgh: The Board of Education and Publication, Reformed Presbyterian Church of North America, 1998).

> This is a well-done psalter that often has multiple versions of the same psalms or lengthier psalms divided into smaller sections. You can find all the tunes for this psalter at www.psalter.com, which is a great aid for personal or family devotions. This version is set up like a hymnal,

which means it has the music and words together for those of you who can read music.

The Psalter: With Doctrinal Standards, Liturgy, Church Order, and Added Chorale Section (Grand Rapids: Reformation Heritage Books, 1999).

This classic psalter dates back to 1893, when the United Presbyterian Church in North America initiated a nine-denominational effort to produce a metrical version of the Psalms. It features a rich array of tunes, often offering several versions of particular psalms. Also helpful is a chorale section, which includes English translations with Genevan tunes from Calvin's *Genevan Psalter.* It presents both words and music, which is helpful for those who read music.

CHAPTER 1

Song of the Righteous Man

Blessed is the man
Who walks not in the counsel of the ungodly,
   Nor stands in the path of sinners,
   Nor sits in the seat of the scornful;
But his delight is in the law of the LORD,
And in His law he meditates day and night.
                                    —PSALM 1:1–2

Today we live in a world full of choices. If you go into a computer store, for example, you can purchase a computer and outfit it with numerous features and options. You can tailor-fit the product to meet your specific needs and demands. Another example of today's seemingly endless choices is the Internet. Millions of Internet surfers have dozens, if not hundreds, of different websites that they have bookmarked in their browsers that give them numerous choices for reading, entertainment, education, and productivity. In this world of many choices, however, Psalm 1 presents a far different picture. Rather than give us multiple choices, the psalmist offers only two: the way of the righteous and the way of the wicked. We often hear that the world is not black and white and that there are many gray areas, but the psalmist entertains no such ideas.

He presents the two ways and, in a sense, introduces a conflict between them and the people who choose them throughout the rest of the Psalter.

The first psalm is one of the few in Book 1 that indicates no author (the same is true for Psalm 2). Nevertheless, it serves as the "foyer" to the "mansion" of the Psalter. Its words represent the attitude with which and method of how the reader should approach the rest of the Psalter. It functions much like the closing words of the book of Ecclesiastes: "Let us hear the conclusion of the whole matter: Fear God and keep His commandments, for this is man's all" (Eccl. 12:13). The first psalm gives a description of two ways: righteousness and wickedness. As we take a closer look, we will learn about the two ways and, more specifically, the way of the righteous man. An important question is, who is the righteous man?

The Two Ways

In verse 1, the psalm begins with a description of the blessed man:

> Blessed is the man
> Who walks not in the counsel of the ungodly,
> Nor stands in the path of sinners,
> Nor sits in the seat of the scornful.

The psalmist tells us that a person can be blessed as he steers clear of ungodliness and wickedness. In his famous book *The Screwtape Letters*, C. S. Lewis characterizes the road to hell as a gradual decline rather than a cliff face, and similarly, the psalmist presents a gradual descent into evil. Notice that the blessed man does not walk, stand, or sit with the wicked, sinners, or scoffers. In other words, a person's engagement with the wicked begins as he walks with them, becomes more involved as he stands with them, and finally results in a close relationship as he sits down with them.

Imagine you are walking along the road with someone who strikes up a conversation with you. You are intrigued, so you stop to consider the substance of the conversation. You want to contemplate the ideas under consideration, so you sit down with your companion, perhaps to share a meal. This illustrates the progression of the way of the wicked. Over the years I have heard confessions from a number of people both within the church and in the broader media who testify that they never thought they would be neck-deep in the sin they were in. They began in a seemingly innocent manner, only to find themselves later drowning in their sin. One public example of this is convicted and executed serial murderer Ted Bundy. In terms of the psalm, he walked with the wicked through dalliances with pornography and ended up sitting with the scoffers through serial murder and rape. The blessed man, then, steers clear of evil, but this is only half the equation.

Notice verse 2: "But his delight is in the law of the LORD, and in His law he meditates day and night." The blessed man, or as verse 6 describes him, the righteous man, takes great delight in the law of Yahweh. Keep in mind that in this context the word *law* means "instruction," or "teaching." Not only does the righteous man delight in the instruction of the Lord but he also constantly sets it before his mind, relentlessly meditating upon it. Not only does he meditate upon it but he also makes it the subject of prayer.

The Lord's instruction and the righteous man's meditation upon it yield fruit, as we see in verse 3:

> He shall be like a tree
>> Planted by the rivers of water,
>> That brings forth its fruit in its season,
>> Whose leaf also shall not wither;
> And whatever he does shall prosper.

The psalmist uses a simile, a comparison of two unlike things (a man and a tree), to describe the prosperity of the righteous man. We must note two things about the prosperity of the righteous man. First, it is the consequence of and not the reward for his delight in the Lord. When a tree is nourished, it naturally produces fruit. Likewise, when the righteous man is nourished by the Lord's instruction, the natural consequence is the fruit of righteousness.

Second, we must not understand the prosperity of the righteous man in some sort of crass, materialistic fashion —the psalmist is not writing about the health and wealth gospel or an abundance of wealth or material possessions such as cars, money, and large mansions. Rather, this prosperity must be understood in the light of the rest of Scripture, which I will explain later in the chapter. We need to understand, however, that the psalmist's use of the simile of the fruitful tree suggests that meditation upon God's instruction does not necessarily produce immediate results.

Rather, just as a tree must be planted and grow for a time before it yields fruit, so also the righteous man's prayerful meditation upon the law of the Lord eventually yields a bounty. As one author writes:

> The habit of prayer, this incessant meditation on God's Law, is not supposed to be something immediately useful. Trees do not bear fruit right away. They first must eat amply of the earth and drink deeply of its water. Such nourishment must serve first to build up the tree. The fruit will come later on, when it is supposed to. The life of Christian prayer and meditation knows nothing of instant holiness; it is all a matter of perseverance and patience. Some trees do not even begin to bear fruit for many years.[1]

In contrast, the psalmist tells us in verse 4 that because the wicked hate the instruction of the Lord, they are blown about like chaff—the leftover bits of the harvest.

So, then, what awaits the wicked, those who hate the law of God? The psalmist writes: "Therefore the ungodly shall not stand in the judgment, nor sinners in the congregation of the righteous" (v. 5). The psalmist looks to the future, to the final judgment, and explains that those who hate God will not stand in the judgment. Nor will the wicked be found in the midst of the congregation of the righteous, the people of God. Verse 6 presents a contrast: "For the LORD knows the way of the righteous, but the way of the ungodly shall perish." This means that the Lord knows the destiny of the righteous; therefore,

---

1. Patrick Henry Reardon, *Christ in the Psalms* (Ben Lomond, Calif.: Conciliar Press, 2000), 2.

He protects them and brings them to that destination. At the final judgment He acknowledges them as His people, whereas the wicked, the psalmist tells us, will perish.

Who Is the Righteous Man?

As we reflect upon what the psalmist has written, we see that he clearly presents the two ways—the way of the righteous and the way of the wicked. He showcases the characteristics of both the righteous and the wicked man. However, as I asked at the beginning of the chapter, who is the righteous man? Do we too quickly read the psalm and think that *we* are the righteous man? Perhaps in the effort to be egalitarian and "improve" the Bible and its patriarchal views, many translations render the opening verse, "Blessed are those..." which is a distortion of what the text says. To translate the passage in this manner changes the rest of the message. How? In this way: both the Hebrew and Greek words used for *man* are not the generic terms that denote human beings. Rather, there is one particular man in view. Who is he? The second psalm gives a further hint.

We often make the mistake of identifying only some of the psalms as messianic, such as 2, 22, and 110. Instead, we must identify *all* of the psalms as messianic—they all point us to Christ. Jesus told His disciples on the road to Emmaus: "These are the words which I spoke to you while I was still with you, that all things must be fulfilled which were written in the Law of Moses and the Prophets and the Psalms concerning Me" (Luke 24:44). This means that Jesus is the righteous and blessed man. Not only does the broader witness of Scripture confirm this but also the immediate context.

Interpreters from the earliest days, both Jewish and Christian, have noted that Psalms 1 and 2 are supposed to be taken together as one literary unit. Psalm 1 begins by talking about the blessing that falls upon *the* blessed man (v. 1), and Psalm 2 ends with the blessing that falls upon all who take refuge in the Messiah (v. 12). Psalm 2 is clearly about the Messiah, the Anointed of God. If we put these two psalms together, then (remember, there were no chapter divisions in the Bible—they were added long after the Bible was written), the psalmist informs us that the Messiah, Jesus, is the blessed and righteous man.

Think of it! Can Adam, Abraham, Moses, David, Solomon, or any other Old Testament saint lay claim to the title that he is *the* righteous man? How is anyone righteous? The answer comes from the earliest chapters of the Bible when God declared Abraham righteous by faith in the promise of the Redeemer to come—because of his faith in Jesus (Gen. 15:6). Christ was the One who did not walk, stand, or sit in the counsel, path, or seat of the wicked. Christ delighted Himself in the law of His heavenly Father; not only was He completely obedient to it but he also meditated upon it day and night. Jesus told His disciples: "My food is to do the will of Him who sent Me, and to finish His work" (John 4:34).

We frequently see Jesus withdrawing from the crowds and His disciples so that He could pray and meditate upon the instruction of His Father. Indeed, Jesus is like a tree that is planted by streams of water that yields its fruit in season. It is crucial that we see this because if we miss it, we will fail to see the source of our salvation, life, and sanctification. We cannot and will not become righteous by meditating upon the instruction of the Lord. We are, in and of ourselves, incapable of being righteous—we have no righteousness of which to speak. To come to the Word of God apart from the mediatorial work of Christ and the power of the Holy Spirit is to try to feed ourselves when we do not have a mouth. What does the psalmist say? Blessed are all those who take refuge in the Messiah (2:12).

We must, therefore, look to Christ by faith alone, as not only will Christ, the one righteous man, save us from our sins but He will also fill us with the Holy Spirit and enable us to be like that tree planted by streams of water that yields its fruit in its season. Only in Christ, by the power of the Spirit, can we approach the instruction of the Lord and delight in it. Only in Christ, the righteous man, can we produce fruit like the tree planted by streams of water. Recall Jesus' words in John 15:4–5: "Abide in Me, and I in you. As the branch cannot bear fruit of itself, unless it abides in the vine, neither can you, unless you abide in Me. I am the vine, you are the branches. He who abides in Me, and I in him, bears much fruit; for without Me you can do nothing." Therefore, beloved, look to Christ by faith, meditate upon His Word, and pray to Christ that He would manifest His righteousness in you.

Remember, as the tree requires time to produce fruit, our sanctification will not be instantaneous. Rather, sometimes we will struggle with our sins for a while. However, we must begin by confessing our sinfulness, whatever it might be, and patiently wait on Christ to conform us to His image. At the same time, we must fill our hearts with

His Word and meditate upon it day and night. We must not walk in the counsel of the wicked, stand in the way of sinners, or sit in the seat of scoffers. Apart from Christ, we will undoubtedly begin the descent into such sinful conduct. Therefore, we must constantly seek refuge in Him.

Conclusion

I close this chapter with a portrait that will help us see Psalm 1 in the light of Christ. In the garden-temple of Eden, the first Adam stood in the presence of God, his Father, in the midst of a grove of fruit-bearing trees. In subsequent temples, the high priest would stand in the presence of God, his Father, as he was flanked by the temple menorah, a lighted almond tree, and later golden palm trees that were etched into the walls of the temple.

Psalm 92:12–15 likens the righteous people of God, like Psalm 1, to trees, but more specifically to palm trees:

> The righteous shall flourish like a palm tree,
> He shall grow like a cedar in Lebanon.
> Those who are planted in the house of the LORD
> Shall flourish in the courts of our God.
> They shall still bear fruit in old age;
> They shall be fresh and flourishing,
> To declare that the LORD is upright;
> He is my rock, and there is no unrighteousness
> in Him.

Here the psalmist paints a prophetic picture of the future that looks just like the prophetic architecture and accoutrements of the tabernacle and temple. What was that prophetic portrait?

To what does Jesus liken the godly person but a fruitful tree? In Luke 6:43–44 He says, "For a good tree does not bear bad fruit, nor does a bad tree bear good fruit. For every tree is known by its own fruit. For men do not gather figs from thorns, nor do they gather grapes from a bramble bush." This imagery reappears in the closing chapters of the Bible and symbolizes none other than Jesus Christ, our Great High Priest, the last Adam, who stands in the midst of His heavenly Father surrounded by the saints, the righteous people of God, those who are planted by the river of life and yield the fruit of the Spirit in season. Rejoice that Jesus Christ is the blessed and righteous man and that He—by His life, death, resurrection, and ascension—makes us what we have been declared by faith alone in Him: a righteous and fruit-bearing people.

▶ **Questions for Further Study**

1. Why is it incorrect to translate Psalm 1:1 as "Blessed are those…," or "Blessed are the people…"?

2. Find another biblical passage that, like Psalm 1, describes the gentle and gradual descent into sin.

3. Who is the righteous man of Psalm 1?

4. How do we receive the blessings of Psalm 1 since we are sinful?

5. Explain the narrative connections between Psalms 1 and 2. How are they linked?

▶ Metrical Version of Psalm 1

Arlington, C.M.

O greatly blessed is the man
Who walketh not astray
In counsel of ungodly men,
Nor stands in sinners' way,

Nor sitteth in the scorner's chair,
But placeth his delight
Upon God's law, and meditates
On His law day and night.

He shall be like a tree that grows
Set by the water side,
Which in its season yields its fruit,
And green its leaves abide;

And all he does shall prosper well.
The wicked are not so,
But are like chaff which by the wind
Is driven to and fro.

In judgment therefore shall not stand
Such as ungodly are,
Nor in th' assembly of the just
Shall wicked men appear.

Because the way of godly men
Is to Jehovah known;
Whereas the way of wicked men
Shall quite be overthrown.

                —*The Book of Psalms for Singing*,
                Psalm 1A

CHAPTER 2

Song of the Lord's Messiah

> *I will declare the decree:*
> *The LORD has said to Me,*
> *"You are My Son,*
> *Today I have begotten You.*
> *Ask of Me, and I will give You*
> *The nations for Your inheritance,*
> *And the ends of the earth for Your possession."*
> —PSALM 2:7–8

In the previous chapter, the psalmist introduced the righteous man, whom we identified as Jesus. Jesus did not walk in the counsel of the wicked, stand in the way of sinners, or sit in the seat of scoffers. Rather, He delighted Himself in the instruction of the Lord, His heavenly Father. This is the chief theme of the first psalm that segues to the themes of the second psalm.

As we begin our study of Psalm 2, it is helpful to think of Jesus' words to His brothers when they mockingly encouraged Him to go to the Feast of Tabernacles and reveal His identity to the world: "My time has not yet come, but your time is always ready. The world cannot hate you, but it hates Me because I testify of it that its works are evil" (John 7:6–7). If we put Jesus' statement to His brothers together with Psalm 1, we see the natural reaction that develops in Psalm 2. In other words, Jesus, the righteous man, contrasts with the world, which is filled with those who hate the instruction of the Lord—the people who walk, stand, and sit in the counsel of the wicked. Jesus' righteousness reveals the wickedness of those in the world, and when He does so, they naturally respond with hatred. In this sense, the contrast between the righteous man and the wicked, the two ways, becomes the messianic conflict in Psalm 2.

Along with the brewing conflict between the righteous man, Jesus, and the unbelieving world arises a second conflict between those who seek shelter in the Messiah and those who refuse Him. Who is victorious in this battle? The psalmist assures us that the victor is the Lord and His Anointed, the Messiah. If we recognize that both Psalms 1 and 2 are about Jesus, then we will see that this passage is a great source of comfort for the church because it offers a christological interpretation of history. It tells us that, ultimately, all of history revolves around the Messiah and His conquest over the wicked, which means victory for those who look to Him by faith.

The Conflict of the Ages

Psalm 2:1–3 describes the messianic conflict between the Lord's Anointed and the nations:

> Why do the nations rage,
> And the people plot a vain thing?
> The kings of the earth set themselves,
> And the rulers take counsel together,

Against the LORD and against His Anointed, saying,
"Let us break Their bonds in pieces
And cast away Their cords from us."

The psalmist presents Jesus, the righteous man, the Lord's Anointed, the *Messiah* (Hebrew), the *Christ* (Greek). Both the Jew and Gentile nations rage against Him and plot in vain. This is the wicked counsel we read about in Psalm 1, the way of sinners and the seat of scoffers.

Think back to the beginning of Christ's ministry. Upon hearing of the birth of Jesus, Herod immediately began to plot against Him. The religious leaders—the Pharisees, Sadducees, and scribes—plotted to kill Jesus. Think of the plotting and machinations of Herod and Pilate, who sought permanently to extinguish the light that the righteous man, Jesus, shone to the entire world. In Acts 4:24–28, the apostles recall this plotting and apply Psalm 2 to the events of Christ's ministry:

> So when they heard that, they raised their voice to God with one accord and said: "Lord, You are God, who made heaven and earth and the sea, and all that is in them, who by the mouth of Your servant David have said: 'Why did the heathen rage, and the people plot vain things?' …For truly against Your holy Servant Jesus, whom You anointed, both Herod and Pontius Pilate, with the Gentiles and the people of Israel, were gathered together to do whatever Your hand and Your purpose determined before to be done.

They recognized that Gentiles and Jews conspired to throw off the rule of Yahweh and His Anointed.

The Lord's Response

But what was the Lord's reaction? The psalmist writes: "He who sits in the heavens shall laugh; the Lord shall hold them in derision" (v. 4). Imagine an anthill teeming with thousands of diminutive creatures as they try to mount an assault upon the gardener; such an idea is laughable. The gardener can flood the anthill with water or douse it with poisonous chemicals or flames. In similar fashion, the Lord sits in the heavens and laughs at the attempts of sinful man to overthrow His rule and the reign of His Anointed. And in response to their rebellion, the Lord instead speaks to them in His wrath and fury and defiantly installs His Anointed upon Zion, His holy mountain and dwelling place (vv. 5–6).

What does the Lord say? In verse 7, He announces the inauguration of the reign of the Messiah:

"I will declare the decree:
The LORD has said to Me,
'You are My Son;
Today I have begotten You.'"

We must understand that when the Lord says, "Today I have begotten You," it does not mean that there was a point when the Son did not exist. The Son of God is eternal, as the first chapter of John's gospel clearly tells us (vv. 1–3). The Lord says, "You are My Son," not, "You will be My Son." In what way, then, is the Messiah begotten?

This is royal ascension language—what is said of a person who enters the royal palace as an ordinary man and leaves as an ascended and inaugurated king. We might say the same thing of the inauguration of our own president. Before the ceremony, he is a regular citizen, but after his inauguration on the Capitol steps, he is president of the United States. In this sense, the nation begets a president. This is how we must understand David's statement. But the question remains: When was Jesus inaugurated and installed on Mount Zion, God's holy hill? The apostle Paul explains this part of the psalm:

> God raised [Jesus] from the dead. He was seen for many days by those who came up with Him from Galilee to Jerusalem, who are His witnesses to the people. And we declare to you glad tidings— that promise which was made to the fathers. God has fulfilled this for us their children, in that He has raised up Jesus. As it is also written in the second Psalm:
>
> > "You are My Son,
> > Today I have begotten You." (Acts 13:30–33)

Paul identifies the resurrection of Jesus as His royal enthronement.

Along with His resurrection, we should connect Jesus' ascension to sit at the right hand of God with His enthronement. We must recognize, though, that the context of Paul's explanation was that the church was undergoing persecution and sought shelter in the present reign of the Messiah. The nations hatched their plots and their schemes, yet the Lord sits in heaven and laughs. The wicked put Jesus to death, but God defiantly raised Him from the dead and seated Him at His right hand, which in effect reversed the unjust verdict and execution of His Son at the hands of wicked men.

At the right hand of the Father, Jesus then received an inheritance, which the psalmist describes in verses 8–9:

> "'Ask of Me, and I will give You
> The nations for Your inheritance,
> And the ends of the earth for Your possession.
> You shall break them with a rod of iron;
> You shall dash them to pieces like a potter's vessel.'"

Even though Christ has been installed on Mount Zion, the nations still conspire and rebel against His authority as they walk in the counsel of the wicked, stand with sinners, and sit in the seat of scoffers. For their rebellion, the Messiah will come with a rod of iron and a sword and bring destruction upon them. Note how John describes the return of Christ in the book of Revelation: "Now out of His mouth goes a sharp sword, that with it He should strike the nations. And He Himself will rule them with a rod of iron. He Himself treads the winepress of the fierceness and wrath of Almighty God" (Rev. 19:15). Why, however, does John say that the sword comes from the Messiah's mouth, probably conjuring odd imagery that we might not necessarily understand?

If we realize that Christ's Word, the gospel, is a double-edged sword, then it is through the proclamation of the gospel that Christ brings the nations under judgment, even at this moment. But does this mean that there is no escape from the wrath of God and the sword of His Anointed? Will all people fall under the just condemnation of the Anointed King for their rebellion and sin? There is an escape from this just wrath for the wise kings and judges of the earth:

> Serve the LORD with fear,
> And rejoice with trembling.
> Kiss the Son, lest He be angry,
> And you perish in the way,
> When His wrath is kindled but a little.
> Blessed are all those who put their trust in Him.
>   (vv. 11–12)

The psalmist exhorts the kings of the earth to be wise. But what is wisdom? The author of Proverbs reminds us that "the fear of the LORD is the beginning of wisdom" (9:10). If the kings of the earth are wise, they will submit to the authority of the Christ.

David calls the wicked kings and rulers to abandon their rebellious plans, which serve their corrupt ends, and to serve the Lord with fear and trembling. He therefore calls the wicked to repent. Not only must they abandon their sinful plans but they must also kiss the Son because in the Bible, and in this setting, to kiss the Son is to show submission to Him. When Samuel anointed David to be king of Israel, he immediately embraced and kissed him: "Then Samuel took a flask of oil and poured it on his head, and kissed him and said: 'Is it not because the LORD has anointed you commander over His inheritance?'" (1 Sam. 10:1). Samuel submitted to the authority of the Lord's anointed—King David. But now David calls the nations to kiss the Son, the Messiah, to submit to the reign and authority of Jesus. Those who refuse to bow the knee, such as those who follow the way of the wicked in Psalm 1, will perish. But those who submit to the Son, who kiss Him, will find refuge and peace.

David's words are not simply those of an ancient prophecy that has never come to pass or that is true but has yet to be fulfilled. These are ancient words, written long ago, that were fulfilled in the first advent of Christ, chiefly in Jesus' resurrection and ascension. The nations plotted in vain to throw off the authority of God and His Anointed, but the Lord sat in the heavens and laughed and raised His Son from the dead and has made him King of kings and Lord of lords. In the words of Scripture made famous by Handel's *Messiah*: "The kingdoms of this world have become the kingdoms of our Lord and of His Christ, and He shall reign forever and ever!" (Rev. 11:15). This means that David's counsel is as relevant as ever, as the nations still rage and the peoples still plot in vain. Sinful man continues to think he can throw off the bonds of the authority of the Lord and His Christ. This plotting is evident in the world's persecution of the church.

Paul and the apostles sought shelter in the hope of Psalm 2 when the Jewish leaders persecuted and opposed them. When we find ourselves suffering for the sake of righteousness or when the church suffers persecution, we too must seek shelter in the hope of this psalm. However, we would be mistaken if we think that David's message applies only to the powerful, only to kings and princes such as Herod and Pilate and the Jewish authorities. Rather, David's call to repentance goes out to the entire world, to people of high and mean estates, to the wealthy and poor, men and women, young and old, Jew and Gentile, free and slave. This was the message of John the Baptist and Jesus: "Repent, for the kingdom of heaven is at hand!" (Matt. 3:2). The Messiah sits upon the throne of God's kingdom, but His kingdom is no longer at hand. It is here! We must therefore repent of our rebellion and sin and kiss the Son.

For some, submission to Christ means to surrender, repent, and confess their sinfulness and seek shelter in the Messiah, in Jesus—to trust in His life, death, resurrection, and ascension as that which saves sinners from the wrath of God. For those of us who have already professed our faith in Christ, submission means searching our hearts and asking whether we harbor sin in our lives. Is there any area of our lives that we hold as a bastion to our own rule? Many Christians trust Christ with the conquest of death and eternal life, but they are hesitant to trust Him with their lives on a day-in, day-out basis. In other words, we are prepared to trust Christ for eternal life, but we are not so sure about tomorrow. Pray that the Holy Spirit would reveal to you those areas in your life where you refuse to submit to Christ's authority. However, there is a message of hope in this passage, just as it was a source of hope for the persecuted church in the days of the apostles.

So often we look out at the world and wonder whether God is truly in control, as it sometimes seems as though chaos reigns rather than Christ. This is especially the case when Christians around the world suffer at the hands of the unbelieving world. Yet remember what this psalm tells us about the christological understanding of the history of the world. Try as they might, the nations cannot and will not overthrow the reign of the Lord and His Anointed. Not only will they not overthrow the reign of the Messiah but also, in spite of the world's efforts, Christ will preserve all who seek shelter in Him. As the apostle John writes: "And he who overcomes, and keeps My works until the end, to him I will give power over the nations—'He shall rule them with a rod of iron; They shall be dashed to pieces like the potter's vessels'—as I also have received from My Father" (Rev. 2:26–27). John echoes the words of Psalm 2 and applies them to the church, to those who seek shelter in the Messiah. What is said of the Messiah is also true of those who take shelter in Him. To be joined to the Head is to be the body of Christ, and this means not only that we reign and rule now with Him as we are seated with Him in the heavenly places but also that our reign will be completely realized at the consummation when Christ returns.

Conclusion

We must repent of our sinful ways, kiss the Son, and seek refuge in Him. But we should also rejoice that the blessed and righteous man of Psalm 1 is also the Messiah, the Lord's Anointed, of Psalm 2, the only begotten Son of God, the only Mediator between God and man, who now reigns and rules on high.

▶ **Questions for Further Study**

1. How is the obedience of the righteous man (Jesus) of Psalm 1 connected to the enthronement of the Messiah in Psalm 2? See Philippians 2:5–11.

2. What does the title *Christ* mean?

3. When does the reign of the Messiah begin?

4. Why did the early church find hope in the message of Psalm 2 in the face of persecution?

5. How does the apostle John apply this psalm to believers?

▶ Metrical Version of Psalm 2

Saxony, L.M.

O wherefore do the nations rage,
And kings and rulers strive in vain,
Against the Lord of earth and heav'n
To overthrow Messiah's reign?

Their strength is weakness in the sight
Of him who sits enthroned above;
He speaks, and judgments fall on them
Who tempt his wrath and scorn his love.

By God's decree his Son receives
The nations for his heritage;
The conqu'ring Christ supreme shall reign
As King of kings, from age to age.

Be wise, ye rulers of the earth,
And serve the Lord with godly fear;
With rev'rent joy confess the Son
While yet in mercy he is near.

Delay not, lest his anger rise,
And ye should perish in your way;
Lo, all that put their trust in him
Are blest indeed, and blest alway.

—*Trinity Hymnal: Revised Edition*, no. 314

CHAPTER 3

Song of Deliverance

> *But You, O LORD, are a shield for me,*
> *My glory and the One who lifts up my head.*
> *I cried to the LORD with my voice,*
> *And He heard me from His holy hill.*
> —PSALM 3:3–4

At this point in the Psalter, the last thing we might expect is a descent into suffering. After all, Psalm 1 spoke of the righteous man and the blessings he receives and the judgment of the wicked. Psalm 2 extends this imagery by identifying the righteous man as the Messiah, the One who was enthroned and inaugurated as king because of His obedience. Think, for example, of the apostle Paul's description of Christ's ministry and how it echoes the pattern found in Psalms 1 and 2:

> Let this mind be in you which was also in Christ Jesus, who, being in the form of God, did not consider it robbery to be equal with God, but made Himself of no reputation, taking the form of a bondservant, and coming in the likeness of men. And being found in appearance as a man, He humbled Himself and became obedient to the point of death, even the death of the cross.

Therefore God also has highly exalted Him and given Him the name which is above every name, that at the name of Jesus every knee should bow, of those in heaven, and of those on earth, and of those under the earth, and that every tongue should confess that Jesus Christ is Lord, to the glory of God the Father. (Phil. 2:5–11)

Psalm 2 and Philippians 2:5–11 highlight the themes of obedience and suffering, though both also end on a triumphant note. And the psalmist, like Paul, paints a portrait of the wicked falling under the Messiah's judgment. But why does the Psalter descend into suffering after rising to a point of victory and triumph? How can it transition from the triumphant inaugural ascent of the Messiah to the descent into darkness and suffering? We find the answer in King David's life, which was prophetic of Christ's.

King David was the anointed of Israel but nonetheless had to flee for his life from Saul and others who persecuted him. In some circumstances, the persecution David experienced was the consequence of his sin; hence, his experience distinctly contrasts with that of his Greater Son, Jesus, who was perfectly sinless. Despite His sinlessness, Jesus, the Messiah, suffered even though He was king, and to this day the church, though it is seated with Christ in the heavenly places and reigns and rules with Him (Eph. 2:6; Col. 3:1–4), still suffers to varying degrees. Such is the pattern that develops as the narrative moves from Psalms 1 and 2 into this third chapter. But before we proceed to see Christ in this psalm, we need to refresh our memories with its historical setting, which the title inscription provides: "A Psalm of David when he fled from Absalom his son."

Among the many events of King David's life, one of the more intense and personally troubling was his flight from Jerusalem when his son Absalom raised up an army against him. For many years, King David had ruled in the wake of his adultery with Bathsheba; his murder of her husband, Uriah the Hittite; and his ensuing deceptive plot to cover up his sin. Like a virus that quickly spread throughout a weakened body, David's kingdom was infected by his sin. His son Absalom began to sin in grievous ways. First, he sought vengeance against his brother Amnon because he had violated Absalom's sister Tamar (2 Sam. 13:1–22). So Absalom looked for an opportune moment and killed his brother in vengeance (2 Sam. 13:23–33).

Not satisfied with taking vengeance, Absalom began to plot against his father. He sat at the gates of Jerusalem and began to win over the people's hearts by telling them that King David was not interested in their troubles, but he would solve them. After four years of currying favor with the people, Absalom knew the time was ripe, so he plotted a coup d'état and overthrew his father. David's counselors immediately came to him and apprised him of the situation—that a large number of the people now supported Absalom and that he had to flee for his life. David was in dire straits.

Not only was David fleeing from his son, who might assassinate him, but he was also fleeing into exile from the presence of God. The Levites brought the ark of the covenant out to follow David into exile, but David told the high priest: "Carry the ark of God back into the city. If I find favor in the eyes of the LORD, He will bring me back and show me both it and His dwelling place. But if He says thus: 'I have no delight in you,' here I am, let Him do to me as seems good to Him" (2 Sam. 15:25–26). The messiah—the king in exile and on the run from those who seek to kill him—is the context of the third psalm. In what ways is David's flight connected to Jesus? In what ways is David's flight connected to the church? Psalm 3 provides answers to these questions. We will see that when we are in need of rescue, we can turn only to our faithful covenant Lord, even when it appears as if He has abandoned us and we are surrounded by our foes.

David's Cry
The psalm begins with David's cry as he looks around him and flees for his life:

> LORD, how they have increased who trouble me!
> Many are they who rise up against me.
> Many are they who say of me,
> "There is no help for him in God." (vv. 1–2)

We must realize that David's main concern probably was not his son, but those surrounding him. Study the history of revolutions, and you will find that often those who surround leaders can be filled with greater zeal for the cause. In an effort to ingratiate themselves with Absalom, his retinue likely looked for the opportunity to kill King David. What better way to elevate your profile with the new king than to eliminate his greatest enemy? Hence, David cried out to the Lord that his foes were great in number. These foes also mocked David, as the psalm tells us. Perhaps as David fled for his life into exile, people stood by and mocked him and questioned whether he truly was God's anointed.

So often people judge by appearances, and because David was on the run and had been ousted, it appeared to many onlookers, especially those who sought to kill him, that God would not save him. We can begin to answer the first question we posed in the introduction. In what ways is David's flight connected to Jesus? The immediate context of this psalm produces connections to Jesus. Recall that Jesus is the righteous man of Psalm 1 who, because of His obedience, would be installed upon God's holy hill, Mount Zion. In Psalm 3 the battle between God's Anointed, His Messiah, and the wicked is fully underway.

The parallels are not precise—they usually are not— but it was Jesus who was *the* Messiah, and throughout His life there were those who sought to kill Him. Whether it was King Herod, who sought to kill Him soon after His birth, or the religious leaders, who on numerous occasions sought to put Him to death, Jesus was in many ways a king on the run—a king in exile from His throne. The King of kings went into the far country, a land marked by libertine and idolatrous living, to redeem a people for Himself. In fact, the religious leaders uttered words similar to the ones we find here: "He trusted in God; let Him deliver Him now if He will have Him; for He said, 'I am the Son of God.' Even the robbers who were crucified with Him reviled Him with the same thing" (Matt. 27:43–44). In a far greater way than King David, who was exiled from God's presence as He was enthroned upon the ark in the tabernacle, Christ was exiled from God's presence in His crucifixion. The author of Hebrews tells us He was crucified outside the camp, exiled from the benevolent presence of His heavenly Father (13:12). The righteous man, in spite of His perfect obedience, nevertheless suffered the curse of exile for the disobedience of His people.

David's Source of Hope

How might we respond under similar circumstances? Would we abandon all hope? To whom would we turn? If we were king, would we seek to find allies so that we might somehow reclaim the throne of Israel? As we examine verses 3–4 we find David losing neither heart nor faith in his covenant Lord. David called the Lord his "shield," one that surrounded him. He also called the Lord his "glory," the one who lifted his head (v. 3). In David's desperation, he cried out to the Lord, and He answered him from His holy hill (v. 4). We may not realize it, but in the context of the Old Testament, this is an amazing series of statements.

Recall that Old Testament saints primarily knew and experienced God's presence by being in proximity to the tabernacle. To draw near to the Lord meant to draw near to the tabernacle, but David could not do this. He was in exile. Yet even though David was in exile from God's presence in the tabernacle, God continued to make His presence known—He accompanied David and answered him in his desperation. It might not be evident how God answered David's pleas, as the psalmist does not provide an explicit explanation. However, the latter part of the psalm reveals what the Lord's answer was to David's prayers for help.

David's Comfort

We read in verse 5: "I lay down and slept; I awoke, for the LORD sustained me." At first glance, this statement might not appear all that significant, but in reality it shouts volumes. Think of the context: David is on the run—he is fleeing for his life. Sleeping could mean the difference between life and death. Perhaps David was thinking of the incident when he crept into Saul's camp while everyone was asleep. While David and his men could have killed the sleeping king, he refused to strike the Lord's anointed. With his son now hunting him, if he were to let his guard down for one second, it might cost him his life.

Imagine the stress and anguish that were on his heart because his own son, whom he dearly loved, over-threw his rule and wanted him dead. What about David's friends, court, and bodyguard? Might they secretly be loyal to his son? Whom could he trust? To whom could he turn? David's mind could easily have run riot with all of the different possibilities, which would have undoubt-edly contributed to one sleepless night after another until he spiraled out of control into sheer madness. But this was not at all the case. David slept!

The Lord gave him the peace that surpasses all under-standing and comforted him with His presence, which explains David's words—"I slept, I woke again, for the Lord sustained me." God gave David an absolute faith in His care for him, one that points forward to the trust Jesus had in the care of His heavenly Father. In Mat-thew 8:23–27, Jesus and His disciples were in the boat on the Sea of Galilee. As they set sail, Jesus was fast asleep, undoubtedly exhausted from His tireless work with the crowds. However, the sea quickly turned violent to the point where the disciples feared for their lives. Jesus, on the other hand, remained asleep. I believe He was fast asleep because, like David before Him, He trusted in His heavenly Father's care.

Here is Jesus, one in exile in the far country who had no place to lay His head, yet He was peacefully asleep in the caring embrace of His heavenly Father. The confidence the Lord gave David is evident in verse 6: "I will not be afraid of ten thousands of people who have set themselves against me all around." God filled David with courage, even in the face of seemingly insurmountable odds. David could fearlessly look upon his enemies and know that his life was in the Lord's hands.

David's Salvation

David's God-given confidence, however, did not lead him to arrogance but rather to a continued faith in the Lord, evidenced by the closing statement of the psalm in verses 7–8:

> Arise, O LORD;
> Save me, O my God!
> For You have struck all my enemies on the
>   cheekbone;
> You have broken the teeth of the ungodly.
> Salvation belongs to the LORD.
> Your blessing is upon Your people.

David's God-given confidence led him further into the embrace of his covenant Lord, for he knew that not only his salvation but also his present circumstances were in His hands.

David makes a seemingly brutal statement regarding his enemies, namely that God has struck them on the cheek and broken their teeth. If you are hit hard enough in the mouth, you will most surely lose teeth—with a quite literally mind-numbing blow. Anyone who has been a victim of such a blow, or seen it happen to someone else, knows that it is a vicious act, so they have trouble understanding how it fits with the prayers of a righteous man like David. It is also difficult for us to see how this might relate to the Christian life. After all, we are supposed to love our enemies, not pray that God would knock out their teeth! Perhaps for unrelated reasons, you will not find Psalm 3 in some hymnals that include numerous psalms. How then can we pray this prayer with David? How can we sing the words of this psalm in praise to God?

As sinful people we have no right to pray in and of ourselves to God and ask Him to break the teeth of our adversaries. How can we pray for justice when we have received mercy? But once again, this is why we must see the Psalms as pointing to Christ. In Him we are righteous, and in Him and His righteousness we can pray for judgment against our enemies. We can pray against the enemies of God as we remember with the apostle Paul: "For we do not wrestle against flesh and blood, but against principalities, against powers, against the rulers of the darkness of this age, against spiritual hosts of wickedness in the heavenly places" (Eph. 6:12). We can pray, therefore, against Satan and his horde that the Lord would judge him severely and strike them in the mouth and break their teeth.

Striking the enemy in the mouth is especially significant, as it is with the mouth that a person either praises and professes faith in Christ or ridicules and pronounces curses against Him. Satan has sent forth a flood of deception from his mouth and uttered all sorts of blasphemies against the triune God. Therefore, pray that God would strike him in the mouth and break his teeth. But there is also a sense in which we can pray against our earthly enemies in this manner. Though we must be careful in praying against specific individuals, for we seldom know with certainty the state of anyone's soul, we can and most definitely should pray against the unbelieving world in general and against those whose lives reveal a blatant blasphemy and opposition against God and His kingdom. We can pray that God would judge the unrepentant, those known only to Him, with His absolute righteous wrath. While we might find the prospect of such a prayer or song difficult to utter, we must do so not out of vengeance but out of praise.

In other words, we must worship our triune Lord for all of His attributes—His mercy, love, benevolence, and kindness and also His wrath, vengeance, justice, and judgment. If we think that the psalmist's words should never be on our lips, then we fail to see the conflict that the psalmist has painted from the opening of the Psalter. What of those who unrepentantly and irreversibly walk in the counsel of the wicked, who stand in the way of scorners, or sit in the seat of scoffers? What of those who refuse to kiss the Son and serve the Lord with fear and trembling and take refuge in the Anointed? As we pray generally against the unrepentant, at the same time we should pray that God's mercy would fall indiscriminately upon hundreds, thousands, and even millions, so that His just wrath would not fall upon them. Moreover, we should rejoice that God has given us refuge in the embassy of peace, in the life, death, resurrection, and ascension of His Anointed, the Messiah, Jesus the Christ.

With this mind-set, David ends his prayer in the following manner: "Salvation belongs to the LORD. Your blessing is upon Your people" (v. 8). David looked not to his own righteousness but to the Lord and His Messiah. Even in exile, David did not lose hope and looked to the Lord to deliver him in both life and death.

Conclusion

Pray this psalm when you feel as though the enemies of God surround you. Pray this psalm for the persecuted church, as many of our brothers and sisters indeed are surrounded by many foes. Seek shelter in the knowledge that the Christ has lived, suffered, died, and undergone exile from the benevolent presence of God so that we will not have to know this judgment. Sing this psalm as a song of praise as we celebrate the mercy and love of Christ and His righteous judgment against the wicked.

Do not lose heart. Even in the face of your enemies, seek the shelter that only Christ can provide not only from the wrath of God against sin and sinners but also from the seemingly chaotic world and persecution. Like David, pray that God would comfort you through Christ and the presence of the Holy Spirit so that no matter what storms might be about, you will know peace and rest—you will know what it means to lie down, sleep, awaken, and know that Jesus Christ has sustained you. Rejoice, for salvation belongs to the Lord and His Messiah, for indeed blessing be upon us, the people of God.

▶ Questions for Further Study

1. How does David's descent into suffering foreshadow the ministry of Christ?

2. May we ever pray for God's judgment to fall upon a specific person? Why?

3. What does the Lord's Prayer, specifically the phrase "Your kingdom come. Your will be done on earth as it is in heaven" (Matt. 6:10) have to do with judgment upon the wicked as in Psalm 3?

4. In what way was David's peace in the face of trial an answer to his prayers?

▶ **Metrical Version of Psalm 3**
New Britain, C.M.

O LORD, how are my foes increased!
Against me many rise.
How many say,
"In vain for help
He on his God relies!"

You are my shield and glory, LORD;
You lifted up my head.
I cried out, "LORD!"
And from His hill
To me His answer sped.

I lay down, slept, and work again—
The LORD is keeping me.
I will not fear ten thousand men
Entrenched surrounding me.

Arise, O LORD! Save me, my God!
You punish all my foes.
You smite the face of wicked men,
Their teeth break with your blows.

Deliverance is from the LORD,
Salvation His alone!
O let Your blessing evermore
Be on Your people shown!

                    —Psalm 3 in *The Book of Psalms for Singing*

CHAPTER 4

Song of Hope

There are many who say,
"Who will show us any good?"
LORD, lift up the light of Your countenance upon us.
You have put gladness in my heart,
More than in the season that their grain and wine
*   increased.*
I will both lie down in peace, and sleep;
For You alone, O LORD, make me dwell in safety.
—PSALM 4:6–8

In the previous chapter we explored the third psalm, which David composed when he was escaping from his son Absalom and was in exile. Historically, the church has used the third psalm in morning worship and prayer services because it references the morning hours. It is specifically in verse 5 that David writes, "I lay down and slept; I awoke, for the LORD sustained me." In many respects, Psalm 4 is the bookend to the third psalm because its focus is the evening, which is evident in its closing verse: "I will both lie down in peace, and sleep; for You alone, O LORD, make me dwell in safety" (v. 8). David probably uttered the words of this psalm in the evening before he went to sleep.

We do not know much of the specific context of the psalm beyond this general time frame, though once again David finds himself surrounded by wicked men. It seems as though the intention was to show that David began and ended his day in strife, in battle against the wicked. However, no matter the circumstances, David continually cried out to the Lord for help. He saw the Lord as his constant source of comfort and hope, the One to whom he could cry out in the midst of his troubles. But why was he being persecuted?

Ultimately, David belonged to the Lord, and the wicked hated him for it. As we explore this psalm, we will find that it tells us things that Jesus has told His bride, the church, a message to which she must cling in times of persecution and suffering. The psalm also contains important instruction regarding the disposition of our hearts; it is easy to become enraged with a sense of self-worth or arrogance in the face of unjust treatment from others. David therefore writes that we should be angry and not sin. These are important words, as they ultimately speak of Christ and those who are united to Him by faith through the indwelling power and presence of the Holy Spirit.

The psalm begins with David crying out to the Lord—a cry grounded in the important acknowledgment that the Lord is his righteousness: "Hear me when I call, O God of my righteousness! You have relieved me in my distress; have mercy on me, and hear my prayer" (v. 1). The psalmist does not construct his platform for addressing his covenant Lord from a precariously balanced collection of his good works. Rather, David knows that the Lord is his righteousness—the Lord has graciously forgiven him of his sins and imputed the righteousness, or obedience, of the coming Messiah to him. This foundation of God's righteousness allows David boldly to call upon the Lord— to seek relief in the midst of his distress.

David's Cry

As I mentioned, we do not know who David's specific enemies are in Psalm 4 as we do in Psalm 3, but we have some indication of their nature from verse 2:

> How long, O you sons of men,
> Will you turn my glory to shame?
> How long will you love worthlessness
> And seek falsehood?

David asks his enemies how long they will persecute him and take his honor and turn it into shame. How long will they utter empty and vain words? How long will they speak lies about him? Notice the distinct break between David's source of comfort and the knowledge of who he is in his covenant Lord and what his enemies have to say about him.

David's confidence and boldness do not hinge on what his enemies say about him but rather what the Lord says he is. This point is amplified in the next verse: "But know that the LORD has set apart for Himself him who is godly; the LORD will hear when I call to Him" (v. 3). We may not at first realize that this verse is perhaps offensive to contemporary man. Why? David clearly has boldness in approaching the Lord in the midst of his suffering, but he is able to do so because the Lord has not only declared him righteous but has also set apart the godly for Himself. How is this offensive to contemporary man?

Look more closely at the statement. David clearly says, "The LORD will hear when I call to Him." The implicit message here is that the Lord does *not* hear the wicked when they call out to Him. If God has given His righteousness to those who are in covenant with Him, if He has set apart the godly for Himself, it is to them that He listens. God hears the cry of the needy, but He does not hear the prayers of the blatantly wicked or of those who walk in the counsel of the wicked, stand in the way of sinners, and sit in the seat of scorners. He does not hear those who refuse to seek refuge in the Messiah. He does not answer the wicked from His holy hill.

I can restate this point in the light of the New Testament: God hears only the cries and prayers of those who are united to Christ by faith through the indwelling power and presence of the Holy Spirit. God hears the cries of His people because of the perfect righteousness, or obedience, of His only begotten Son, Jesus: "In the days of His flesh, when He had offered up prayers and supplications, with vehement cries and tears to Him who was able to save Him from death,...[He] was heard because of His godly fear" (Heb. 5:7). Therefore, it is not because of our righteousness that we are heard but because of the righteousness of Christ that God listens to our prayers as He listened to David's prayer and not those of his enemies.

Because of the redemption that comes through Christ, God hears those who are found in Him. The book of Proverbs, for example, states: "The LORD is far from the wicked, but He hears the prayer of the righteous" (15:29).

The apostle Peter offers a similar observation: "For the eyes of the LORD are on the righteous, and His ears are open to their prayers; but the face of the LORD is against those who do evil" (1 Peter 3:12). This truth rubs against the grain of our democratically minded culture.

Some people might think, "Why shouldn't all people have equal access to God—whoever He might be—that is, *if* He even exists, right?" Yet man cannot define the terms or the manner in which he deals with or approaches God. God does not negotiate but instead has offered His only begotten Son as a mediator so that sinful man might find shelter in Him from His just wrath for man's sinful conduct. God does not hear those who refuse to submit to the Son—He pays them no mind. He sets apart those who seek shelter in the Messiah. He sanctifies them; they are His holy people. Therefore, God hears them when they call in any circumstance in life, but especially in times of trouble and tribulation.

The wicked inherently know of God's love for His people and therefore despise it, which explains why they malign and persecute David. But Christ, the righteous man of Psalm 1 and the Anointed Son of Psalm 2, has told us the same thing:

> "If the world hates you, you know that it hated Me before it hated you. If you were of the world, the world would love its own. Yet because you are not of the world, but I chose you out of the world, therefore the world hates you. Remember the word that I said to you, 'A servant is not greater than his master.' If they persecuted Me, they will

also persecute you. If they kept My word, they
will keep yours also." (John 15:18–20)

In light of Christ's statement, He is the key to the
Psalter and, indeed, the whole Old Testament. Psalm 4 is
only one verse in the great hymn of Scripture that explicates the nature of the battle between the righteous and
the wicked. The overall message is that the wicked will
persecute the righteous, but those who are in Christ have
their heavenly Father's ear.

David's Reminder

Given the special place that believers have, they easily can
fall into a sense of pride and self-righteous anger. David
tells himself in verses 4–5:

> Be angry, and do not sin.
> Meditate within your heart on your bed, and be still.
> Offer the sacrifices of righteousness,
> And put your trust in the LORD.

There is a place in the Christian's life for righteous anger,
especially in the face of the unbelieving world's persecution. But a fine line separates between righteousness
and unrighteousness—that is, righteous anger and sinful
anger. It is one thing to be angered over the rejection of
the truth of the gospel and over the persecution of the
church, especially when Christians are martyred. It is one
thing to be angered over the world's blasphemy against
God. It is entirely another thing, however, to be filled with
anger and indignation because *we* have been offended.

When we move the fulcrum of our anger from Christ to ourselves, we cross the line of righteous anger to sinful self-righteous anger. This is why David writes of offering right sacrifices. He is not saying, "I will offer the right sacrifices to ingratiate myself with God." Rather, he is telling us to offer the right sacrifices so that we maintain a Christ-focused center of gravity. In offering sacrifices, David could not help but see his sin and his need for forgiveness as well as the foreshadow of the once-for-all perfect sacrifice of the Lord's Anointed, Jesus.

David was not the only one to say this. In the light of Christ, we find David's point elaborated and expanded in Paul's letter to the Ephesians:

> That you put off, concerning your former conduct, the old man which grows corrupt according to the deceitful lusts, and be renewed in the spirit of your mind, and that you put on the new man which was created according to God, in true righteousness and holiness.
>
> Therefore, putting away lying, "Let each one of you speak truth with his neighbor," for we are members of one another. "Be angry, and do not sin": do not let the sun go down on your wrath, nor give place to the devil. (4:22–27)

Both David and Paul ground our spiritual ability in our union with Christ, not in ourselves isolated from Christ. In our union with Christ, we receive our "new man," as Paul tells us, whereby we receive the ability to turn away from our sinful anger. We are new creatures in Him by the sanctifying power of the Holy Spirit and thereby can see our anger, turn from it, repent, and instead show love and patience. We should pay attention to the time element of these instructions, especially as it relates to Psalm 3. David began his day in Psalm 3 with the acknowledgment that the Lord sustained him in his sleep, and he ends his day in prayer, asking the Lord to keep him from sinful anger because of the day's events. But David's prayer does not end here.

David's Peace

David's enemies taunt and ask, "Who will show us any good?" to which David calls out: "LORD, lift up the light of Your countenance upon us" (v. 6). David echoes the Aaronic blessing:

> "The LORD bless you and keep you;
> The LORD make His face shine upon you,
> And be gracious to you;
> The LORD lift up His countenance upon you,
> And give you peace." (Num. 6:24–26)

The peace that David knows from God's presence, even in the face of his taunting enemies and in exile from the tabernacle, is one that leads to both blessing and peace. David can say that he has more joy in his heart than the wicked do when their bellies and storehouses are full of grain and wine (v. 7).

As he experienced it in Psalm 3, once again David knows the Lord's peace, to the extent that he can lay his head down and fall asleep once again: "I will both lie down in peace, and sleep; for You alone, O LORD, make me dwell in safety" (v. 8). In our lives we have the same hope in the peace that God gives us in our rest in the midst of trials and persecution. We have had the light of God's face fall upon us in the light of Christ's face. Apart from the light of Christ, we would neither see the kingdom of God nor believe in Jesus. Granted, we cannot behold the physical face of Christ, but we can behold His face with the eyes of faith as we read about Him and His work on our behalf in the pages of Holy Writ. We can physically listen to Him with our ears as we hear the reading and preaching of the Word and look upon Him as we see Him in the sacraments of baptism and the Lord's Supper. We look upon the broken body of Christ in the bread and His shed blood in the wine and behold the outpouring of the Spirit in baptism.

But we will see the face of God in the face of Christ when we ultimately fall asleep in death: "And there shall be no more curse, but the throne of God and of the Lamb shall be in it, and His servants shall serve Him. They shall see His face, and His name shall be on their foreheads" (Rev. 22:3–4). This was the hope that gave David peace in the face of persecution and trial, and even death. Hope in the Messiah, the reigning Anointed Son of Psalm 2, gave him the peace to lay his head down and fall asleep even when he was surrounded by his enemies.

Conclusion

When you find yourself in the midst of trials or distress, perhaps under the cascading words of naysayers who question the existence and benevolence of the God you serve, know that you have the ear of the Creator of heaven and earth. Your heavenly Father stoops to hear your cries and answer your prayers, not because of your obedience or righteousness but because of *His* righteousness—the righteousness He has given you by His grace alone in Christ alone by faith alone.

If the One who fashioned galaxies and worlds of beauty and grandeur beyond our wildest imaginations will listen to us, then why do we fail to cry out to Him in times of need? Why do we turn to others when only God can answer our prayers? But as we rejoice and take refuge in our ability to enter boldly into the presence of God through Jesus, our Mediator, in the power of the Holy Spirit, we must pray that Christ would keep us humble. We can all too quickly forget that we are the recipients of God's grace. We must pray that the knowledge of who we are in Christ would not lead us to be puffed up with pride but instead to be edified in greater humility. And in that humility we should be filled with hope, knowing that though things may appear as if we are forgotten, all is not lost. With our hope anchored firmly in Christ, who sits at the right hand of the Father, we should rejoice in the knowledge that one day we will behold the face of God in the face of Christ. Therefore we must rest each night in the knowledge of the hope that we receive in Christ through the Spirit.

▶ **Questions for Further Study**

1. How are Psalms 3 and 4 connected?

2. How might God's favor lead us to become arrogant?

3. What is the difference between righteous and sinful anger?

4. Who is the source of our ability to express righteous anger?

▶ Metrical Version of Psalm 4

Penitence, 11.11.11.11 (Trochaic)

Answer when I call,
O God who justifies.
In my stress You freed me;
Hear in grace my cries.
Sons of men, how long will
You my glory shame?
Will you love what's worthless?
Will lies be your aim?

Know the LORD His saints
Has set apart in grace,
And the LORD will hear me
When I seek his face.
Tremble in your anger,
Yet from sin depart.
On your bed in silence
Speak within your heart.

May you sacrifice now
Sacrifices just,
In Jehovah only
Placing all your trust.
"Who will show us goodness?"
Many people say;
The light of Your face, LORD,
Lift on us, we pray.

You have given my heart
Greater joy by far
Than when grain and new wine
Most abundant are.

So in peace I lie down;
I will rest and sleep,
For, O LORD, You only
Will me safely keep.

> —*The Book of Psalms for Singing*,
> Psalm 4B

CHAPTER 5

Song of Protection

But let all those rejoice who put their trust in You;
Let them ever shout for joy, because You defend them;
Let those also who love Your name
Be joyful in You.
For You, O LORD, will bless the righteous;
With favor You will surround him as with a shield.
—PSALM 5:11–12

Like Psalm 4, Psalm 5 is a personal lament. Also like the
previous psalm, we do not know the exact context as we
do with Psalm 3 when David was fleeing from Absalom.
But we do know that David is distressed at the words of
the wicked; as in the previous psalms, they are persecuting
him. Despite the old children's taunt, "Sticks and stones
may break my bones, but words will never hurt me," the
truth is that words can have a powerful effect on us, especially lies and deception. Words have the power to edify,
but lies can destroy careers and reputations and leave a
wake of personal destruction.

In the midst of our persecutions and trials, we should
consider where we should flee. Where do we find peace
and refuge? Too often we find solace and refuge in a number of different things. Some of us withdraw and close in

on ourselves—we hide in an emotional cocoon. Others seek shelter in the comfort and encouragement of others; as long as our friends tell us everything is all right, we are content. Or perhaps we take matters into our own hands—we strike back in anger at those who attack us in an effort to outmatch their verbal assault. These are some of the different reactions we might choose, but we find that David looks in another direction.

David looks to the Lord. What might be surprising to some, however, is that David does not approach the Lord in arrogance or pride, but in humility. David knows that the Lord's gracious care is not the result of his righteousness, but God's kindness and grace. In this approach David not only prays against the wicked but that God would have mercy upon him so that he would not become like the wicked. Let's see how David prays, and in his prayer see our need for Christ not only as our comfort and shield in times of trouble but also as our salvation from our own wickedness. Such is the nature of this psalm as it further explicates life in the valley of the shadow of darkness, the descent from the heights of Psalms 1 and 2.

The Cause of David's Cry

This psalm begins like the previous two, with David crying out to the Lord because his foes surround him. In this case, we should notice the intensely personal nature of David's cry in verses 1–2:

> Give ear to my words, O LORD,
> Consider my meditation.
> Give heed to the voice of my cry,

My King, and my God,
For to You I will pray.

Note how many times in these two verses David uses the pronoun *my*. We see that David has an intensely personal relationship with the Lord. His relationship is neither characterized by great emotional distance nor bound exclusively in strict formality. David utters his personal cry to the Creator of the heavens and earth as *his* God.

The personal nature of David's relationship with God is not unique: every person who is joined to Christ by faith knows an even greater intimacy than David: "For as many as are led by the Spirit of God, these are sons of God. For you did not receive the spirit of bondage again to fear, but you received the Spirit of adoption by whom we cry out, 'Abba, Father.' The Spirit Himself bears witness with our spirit that we are children of God" (Rom. 8:14–16).

David's dependence upon his God and king is especially evident in verse 3. He writes that he would pray to the Lord in the morning, which was a part of Israel's morning sacrifice ritual (cf. 2 Kings 3:20). We can observe a pattern in David's life that has been unfolding in Psalms 3 and 4, one that we would probably not find in the lives of many Christians. In Psalm 3:5 David told us that he prayed to the Lord upon waking from his sleep and gave thanks that the Lord had protected him. In Psalm 4:4, David told us that he would pray before he went to sleep that the Lord would keep him from anger. And here again in verse 3 he tells us that he cried out to the Lord in the morning. His life exhibits a continual pattern of morning and evening prayer.

The degree to which we rely upon Christ is likely reflected in the way in which we pray to Him. How many married couples could legitimately claim they are in love if they were never to speak to each other? What would we say of a couple who silently passed each other every time their paths crossed? Would we characterize such a relationship as a healthy one? Would we say it was a good marriage? Yet is this not a picture of many Christians' prayer lives? They claim to love Christ, the church's Bridegroom, but hardly, if ever, spend time in prayer. What would we say if we were asked about our own prayer habits?

- I'm much too tired in the morning—I need time to wake up.
- I'm much too busy during the day—I need time to slow down.
- I'm much too tired in the evening—I need time to rest.

We find time for the things that are important to us. If we do not pray, quite simply, prayer is not important to us—that is the honest, brutal truth. We find time for eating, bathing, working, entertainment, shopping, and spending time with friends. If prayer is important to us, we will make time for it. David, a man after God's own heart, reflected his intimacy with and utter dependence upon the Lord. Whether in the morning or evening, we know what we could find David doing—praying.

The Content of David's Prayer

We know that we would find David in prayer both morning and evening, but what was the content of his prayers? On this particular occasion David prayed against the wicked, his enemies who spoke lies. We again find sentiments that rub against the grain of our sinful victim mentality. Perhaps earlier generations offered the same excuses, but in our day, people frequently excuse their sin for a host of reasons. Criminals are not responsible for their actions—a vicious and unfair system has driven them to crime. People are not responsible for bad parenting; after all, bad parents produce bad children who later become bad parents. This victim mentality leads people to say, "God hates the sin, not the sinner." We try to disassociate the sinful actions that many recognize as wrong from the one who carries them out. Yet how can we separate the sin from the sinner? If sin has somehow pounced unsuspectingly upon a person, then we can legitimately say he is a victim of sin. We would have the right to conclude that God hates the sin and not the sinner. That line of thinking might lead us to say, "God hates the monkey on my back, which, due to no fault of my own, refuses to leave!"

But what is sin? Is it some sort of illness, analogous to a doctor who hates the cancer but loves the patient? This type of thinking does not work. The Scriptures are abundantly clear; we sin because of *our* wicked and sinful desires. Our sinful actions are ultimately the contents of *our* hearts that pour forth from us like an overrun sewer. To this end notice what David writes regarding the wicked in verse 9:

> For there is no faithfulness in their mouth;
> Their inward part is destruction;
> Their throat is an open tomb;
> They flatter with their tongue.

These words should sound familiar to us, as Paul uses them in his own statement regarding man's sinfulness in Romans 3:18: "There is no fear of God before their eyes." Paul uses this language to indicate that sinners without Christ hate God. How do you separate the sin from the sinner in this case? It seems that the sin and the sinner are irrefragably joined since the sinner has a personal hatred for God.

For this reason, there is no neutral ground where God hates the sin but not the sinner. Instead, David writes,

> For You are not a God who takes pleasure in
>   wickedness,
> Nor shall evil dwell with You.
> The boastful shall not stand in Your sight;
> You hate all workers of iniquity.
> You shall destroy those who speak falsehood;
> The LORD abhors the bloodthirsty and deceitful
>   man. (vv. 4–6)

In light of what David tells us about God and evil, God not only hates the sin but He also hates the sinner! Remember, though, that when David says that God hates all evildoers, His hatred is a holy hatred—it is nothing like our sinful hatred. Rather, God's hatred is a manifestation of His perfect justice and holiness—His judgment against the wicked.

Think of it—there is no real problem if God merely hates the sin and not the sinner. Why not simply ignore the sin if it is the real problem? But if God's holy hatred, His just wrath and condemnation, hangs over the sinner's head, then there is a real problem. So David's prayer is quite illuminating in terms of what he has to say about the nature of sinful man. But do not forget, David does not merely observe the wicked; rather, he prays against them in verse 10:

> Pronounce them guilty, O God!
> Let them fall by their own counsels;
> Cast them out in the multitude of their
>   transgressions,
> For they have rebelled against You.

David calls for God's just wrath to fall upon the wicked. This statement confronts us again with the idea that David prays against the wicked, when other passages in Scripture, including words from Christ Himself, clearly tell us to pray for our enemies. How are these two seemingly contradictory ideas resolved?

As I explained in my exposition of Psalm 3, we should always pray for our enemies—that God's grace in Christ would fall upon them and that they would place their faith in Him and repent of their sins. However, in the case of the one who refuses to repent, who will never turn away from his hatred, we can and should pray that God would judge him or her. I previously made two points regarding this type of prayer. First, as a rule, we should not pray for judgment for any specific individual, as we do not know who and when God will save. Second, in the end, our prayer should not be vindictive but ultimately full of praise for all God's attributes, including His wrath and justice. If we worship God for only some of His attributes, such as His love, mercy, and kindness, then we worship a false god, one of our own making, and not the God revealed in Scripture and this psalm.

The absence of this type of prayer softens our conception of God. If we all but forget that God will judge the wicked, if we sand off God's "rough edges," if we seek shelter in the victim mentality about sin, then perhaps we will not pray in this manner. But if we were to utter these types of prayers, perhaps we would be acutely aware of the serious situation that unbelievers face and would pray all the more for the repentance of specific unbelievers. If we somehow think, however, that this type of sentiment is something we find only in the Old Testament, then we should take a closer look at Jesus' words: "I pray for them. I do not pray for the world but for those whom You have given Me, for they are Yours" (John 17:9). Jesus does not intercede on behalf of the wicked but only for those who belong to Him. At His crucifixion Jesus had only words of assurance and blessing for the thief who professed his faith in Christ. He had nothing to say for the thief that reviled Him. Christ's silence was ultimately the deafening roar of condemnation against an unrepentant man.

The Ground of David's Prayer

One last crucial thing to notice is the ground of David's prayer. David does not approach the Lord in his own righteousness or sense of self-worth, but in God's mercy and grace:

> But as for me, I will come into Your house in the
>   multitude of Your mercy;

> In fear of You I will worship toward Your holy
>   temple.
> Lead me, O LORD, in Your righteousness because
>   of my enemies;
> Make Your way straight before my face. (vv. 7–8)

David does not compare his righteousness with the unrighteousness of the wicked and say, "I will enter Your house because of *my* righteousness." Rather, he clearly sees his place in God's presence as one founded upon divinely and freely given grace.

But we must not fail to notice how David and others receive the grace and righteousness of God:

> But let all those rejoice who put their trust in You;
> Let them ever shout for joy, because You defend
>   them;
> Let those also who love Your name
> Be joyful in You.
> For You, O LORD, will bless the righteous;
> With favor You will surround him as with a shield.
>   (vv. 11–12)

These verses speak of believers trusting in the Lord and seeking shelter in Him, the One who defends them from their foes. We have heard this language before, especially as it relates to the Lord's Anointed:

> Kiss the Son, lest He be angry,
> And you perish in the way,
> When His wrath is kindled but a little.
> *Blessed are all those who put their trust in Him.*
>   (Ps. 2:12, emphasis added)

In this regard, the Messiah, Jesus, is a shield and protection for those who seek refuge in Him in more ways than we might realize. By all means, David says that those who seek refuge in the Lord and in Christ should be marked by joy and the praise of God. Why? Because Christ protects them from their foes—He is like the bird that covers its young, spreading His wings over them. He is a shield for the righteous against their foes. But do not fail to see this statement in context. What happens to those who do not seek shelter in Christ? They suffer the wrath of God—He hates the wicked with a holy hatred. In other words, Jesus is a shield not just against the attacks of the wicked but also against the wrath of God. Like a hen covering its young from a massive barn fire, the Lord Jesus covers us with His wings and is our shield (cf. Luke 13:34). He protects us, bears the wrath due to us, and gives us His righteousness so that we can enter boldly into God's presence without fear, knowing all the while that He has forgiven our sins in Christ. These truths should fill your heart with praise and thanksgiving for our triune Lord.

Conclusion

When we read a prayer like David's, many of us shrink back from uttering these words—we genuinely think them strange and incompatible with the God of mercy. At the same time some people shrink from these words because they want to tame the Lion of Judah. They want to turn Him into a domestic house pet, one who loves us but does not have a hint of anger in Him. Yet, we can and must pray with David that God would justly condemn and judge the wicked. To do this reminds us of God's holiness and His righteous hatred against the wicked.

If we pray it from the ground of faith in Christ and not in arrogance or pride, this psalm is a constant reminder of the wrath the Lion of Judah has borne in His own body on the cross, thereby delivering us. But this prayer is also a reminder of the urgency and fervency with which we should pray for those specific unbelievers we personally know. We should pray that they would take refuge in the Messiah—in Jesus. Psalm 5 explicates the just wrath that will fall upon those who refuse to kiss the Son, the Messiah of Psalm 2. But as we pray, morning and evening, before we lie down and when we rise (Pss. 3–4), we will constantly be reminded of God's grace in Christ—that which undergirds our entire lives—the protection that Christ gives not only from the wrath of God but even from our foes. Rejoice and ever sing for joy because God has spread His protection over us. He has covered us with His favor in Christ by the Spirit as with a shield.

▶ **Questions for Further Study**

1. How much time do you spend in prayer? How could your prayer time be improved?

2. Why is God's wrath and judgment against the wicked an important truth to acknowledge, and how does it fuel our own understanding of God's grace as well as motivate our evangelism?

3. How is Psalm 5 connected to Psalm 2?

4. What is the only ground by which we can boldly approach God in prayer?

▶ Metrical Version of Psalm 5
Rehoboth, 7.7.7.7.D. (alt. tune Aberystwth, 7.7.7.7.D)

O Jehovah, hear my words,
To my thoughts attentive be;
Hear my cry, my King, my God,
I will make my prayer to thee.
With the morning light, O Lord,
Thou shalt hear my voice arise,
And expectant I will bring
Prayer as morning sacrifice.

Thou, Jehovah, art a God
Who delightest not in sin;
Evil shall not dwell with thee,
Nor the proud thy favor win.
Evildoers thou dost hate,
Lying tongues thou wilt defeat;
God abhors the man who loves
Violence and base deceit.

In the fulness of thy grace
To thy house I will repair;
Bowing toward thy holy place,
In thy fear to worship there.
Lead me in thy righteousness,
Let my foes assail in vain;
Lest my feet be turned aside,
Make thy way before me plain.

False and faithless are my foes,
In their mouth no truth is found;
Deadly are the words they speak,
All their thoughts with sin abound.

Bring, O God, their plans to naught,
Hold them guilty in thy sight,
For against thee and thy law
They have set themselves to fight.

O let all that trust thy care
Ever glad and joyful be;
Let them joy who love thy Name,
Safely guarded, Lord, by thee.
For a blessing from thy store
To the righteous thou wilt yield;
Thou wilt compass him about
With thy favor as a shield.

—*Trinity Hymnal*, no. 47

CHAPTER 6

Song of Forgiveness

> *O LORD, do not rebuke me in Your anger,*
> *Nor chasten me in Your hot displeasure.*
> *Have mercy on me, O LORD, for I am weak;*
> *O LORD, heal me, for my bones are troubled.*
> *My soul also is greatly troubled;*
> *But You, O LORD—how long?*
>
> —PSALM 6:1–3

With Psalm 6 we encounter the first of seven penitential psalms that give expression to repentance from sin (32, 38, 51, 102, 130, 143). In this psalm David seeks the Lord's mercy following some unidentified sin. Given some of the statements in this psalm, it seems likely that David did not know his sin and that he perhaps committed it in ignorance. Given other statements in verses 2 and 5, the most likely scenario is that David finds himself gravely ill and confesses it could be his illness is a result of his sin. Therefore, we find David crying out to the Lord for His mercy.

Most of us can identify with David at a certain level, because at some point we have been seriously ill—or at least we probably felt that we were. During the long hours we lie in our beds, our minds begin to drift, and in our weakened state we begin to wonder what we did to invite the illness. We might think, "Did I sin? Is God punishing me for something?" In one sense, we can invoke the words of this psalm in such circumstances. We should always be ready to examine ourselves and ask whether we are guilty of sin. But we should exercise caution because sometimes there is not a direct connection between sin and illness. Sometimes Providence brings illness into our lives so that we can manifest the weakness and suffering of Christ and thereby bring glory to God, and not because we are hiding some secret sin. However, the closer we look at this psalm, we must see the important theme of God's wrath. In other words, David's concern is far more serious than simply not feeling his best or experiencing a bout of depression because of some aches and pains. Rather, he is all too aware of the wrath of God against sinners and therefore cries out to Him for mercy.

Psalms 3 and 5 were prayers that contained words of judgment against the wicked, and in Psalm 6 we see the counterbalance in which David turns his focus on his own sinfulness and need for God's mercy in Christ. Psalms 3–5 dealt largely with the enemies of the anointed king of Psalm 2, and this psalm dwells upon the continued need for God's grace and mercy, even for those who have sought shelter in the Messiah and have kissed the Son. However, there are also connections here to David's Greater Son. Often what occurs to David as the messiah and king is a foreshadow of his Greater Son, Jesus, *the* Messiah and *the* King of kings. Let's see, then, David's plea, the connections to his Greater Son, and ultimately our connection to the text through our union with Christ.

David's Plea

The psalm begins with David's plea to the Lord: "O LORD, do not rebuke me in Your anger, nor chasten me in Your hot displeasure" (v. 1). This is the second time that David has mentioned God's wrath, the first in Psalm 2. In Psalm 2, David writes that the wicked will know God's wrath, but in David's cry in Psalm 6, God's wrath is something that he greatly fears. We have to realize that God's wrath is no light matter. It is real, and He reveals it on the earth even now, as Paul tells us in the first chapter of his epistle to Rome: "For the wrath of God is revealed from heaven against all ungodliness and unrighteousness of men, who suppress the truth in unrighteousness" (v. 18). If the mere act of God's revealing His holy presence has caused great saints such as Isaiah to call a curse upon himself (Isa. 6:5), what should we think about the white-hot holy and just wrath of God?

David is overwhelmed with a sense of both God's holiness and His wrath and knows of no other shelter but in God's grace: "Have mercy on me, O LORD, for I am weak; O LORD, heal me, for my bones are troubled" (v. 2). David knows that nothing he can do will merit God's favor and grace; God's grace is precisely that—His demerited favor. In other words, David did not merit God's favor, but neither is His favor unmerited—that is, undeserved. Rather, it is *demerited*, in that David has received God's favor in spite of his demerits, his sins. However, in this verse we also get the first clues about David's situation: it seems he is suffering from some sort of illness. Perhaps an alternative explanation is that David's physical angst is driven by the knowledge of his sin.

Many of us have been physically sick to our stomachs or physically weakened in some other way over a situation in our lives. If such circumstances in life can affect us, then it is within the realm of possibility that David was physically weakened over the knowledge of his sin. Unlike many who seem to be able to sin and give little thought to the gravity of their misconduct, David is acutely aware of God's just wrath against all sinners. We should note that, especially in light of David's prayers against the wicked in Psalms 4 and 5 when he called God's wrath upon them, David knew his place before the Lord—his posture was one of humility.

David did not presume upon the grace of God. He recognized that his own standing before the Lord was entirely by divine mercy. David was intensely aware of God's holiness and His just wrath, so he writes in verses 3–4:

> My soul also is greatly troubled;
> But You, O LORD—how long?
> Return, O LORD, deliver me!
> Oh, save me for Your mercies' sake!

He tells the Lord how greatly troubled his soul is and asks how long the Lord will allow him to flounder. David's fear of God's wrath, however, was shared by his Greater Son, Jesus.

Jesus echoed the words of his earthly ancestor, King David, as He contemplated the wrath of His heavenly Father: "'Now My soul is troubled, and what shall I say? "Father, save Me from this hour"? But for this purpose I came to this hour. Father, glorify Your name.' Then a voice came from heaven, saying, 'I have both glorified it and will glorify it again'" (John 12:27–28).

Unlike Jesus, who immediately received a word of assurance from His heavenly Father, David languished for a while in his own seemingly dark hour. David saw the prospects of God's wrath and his own death, and in his desperation he told the Lord that he would be unable to praise Him were he to descend into the depths of death (v. 5). Death was no friend of David, nor is it the friend of any Christian. Death is our sworn enemy.

So often people try to mitigate the finality of death and come up with euphemisms to lighten the impact, such as "pass away," "kick the bucket," or "buy the farm." Or people try to assuage themselves with saccharine platitudes that though a person is no longer alive, his memory still lives in their hearts. However true it might be that people fondly remember a loved one does not change the fact that the person is dead and decaying in a coffin buried six feet under the earth.

David's Despair

David was well aware of this truth, and it kept him up at night in the grips of despair: "I am weary with my groaning; all night I make my bed swim; I drench my couch with my tears" (v. 6). We should remember, though, that David's despair was not only for God's judgment that could justly fall upon him but also for his own sinfulness. David's disposition is very different from what we commonly find in our day. Augustine once observed: "What is more pitiable than a wretch without pity for himself who weeps over the death of Dido dying for love of Aeneas, but not weeping over himself dying for his lack of love for you, my God, light of my heart, bread of the inner mouth of my soul, the power which begets life in my mind and in the innermost recesses of my thinking."[1] Augustine is referring to Virgil's *Aeneid*, in which Dido, queen of Carthage, falls in love with Aeneas, a Trojan refugee, in what is basically a tragic romance story. Augustine observes that people weep over a fictitious tragic romance story, but they have dry eyes over their lack of love for God. Have you ever wept over a sad movie? How often do you shed a tear over your sin against God? How much do we mourn our sin in comparison to our mourning over the fictional tragedies we are exposed to? Does our quest for the forgiveness of sin remain a cold business transaction? David's own sinfulness and the prospects of God's wrath weighed upon him like the world upon the shoulders of Atlas. However, David was not distraught over these things only. On the one hand, David was distraught over his sin, but on the other hand, his enemies also pressed him. Here Psalm 6 reflects the complexities of life in a sin-fallen world: "My eye wastes away because of grief; it grows old because of all my enemies" (v. 7). David was concerned about his own sin at the same time he was being attacked by his foes.

One possible scenario is that David was seriously ill, and, like Job's friends, his enemies were accusing him of harboring sin. It is also possible that David had indeed sinned and now his enemies were taking advantage of his

---

1. Augustine, *Confessions*, trans. Henry Chadwick (Oxford: Oxford University Press, 1991), 1.13 (21), 15–16.

situation by taunting and persecuting him—telling him how God would never forgive him for his sinful conduct. Regardless of the reasons, David rebukes his enemies and calls again upon the Lord: "Depart from me, all you workers of iniquity; for the LORD has heard the voice of my weeping" (v. 8). Once again, David's Greater Son, Jesus, takes these words upon His lips in His own pronouncement of judgment against the wicked:

> Then one said to Him, "Lord, are there few who are saved?"
>
> And He said to them, "Strive to enter through the narrow gate, for many, I say to you, will seek to enter and will not be able. When once the Master of the house has risen up and shut the door, and you begin to stand outside and knock at the door, saying, 'Lord, Lord, open for us,' and He will answer and say to you, 'I do not know you, where you are from,' then you will begin to say, 'We ate and drank in Your presence, and You taught in our streets.' But He will say, 'I tell you I do not know you, where you are from. *Depart from Me, all you workers of iniquity.*'" (Luke 13:23–27, emphasis added)

David's prayer for deliverance becomes the sentence of condemnation on Christ's lips.

David's Hope
The last thing we should observe about David's prayer is the hope he finds in the Lord. Were we to stop at verse 8, we might think that David ends on a depressing note, as

he simply says that the Lord has heard his weeping but seemingly has not responded. But notice how David concludes the psalm in verses 9–10:

> The LORD has heard my supplication;
> The LORD will receive my prayer.
> Let all my enemies be ashamed and greatly
>   troubled;
> Let them turn back and be ashamed suddenly.

We should notice the tense shift in the verbs in verse 9: "The LORD *has heard*…. The LORD *will receive*." The verbs move from past to future tense. God has heard David's prayers. David is confident that God will answer them. David's enemies will be shamed—it will no longer be David who is greatly troubled, but his enemies.

David's Greater Son

We have already touched briefly on the connection between David and Jesus in this psalm, that Jesus uttered David's cry in verse 3: "My soul also is greatly troubled." This shows us once again that all the psalms are christological. They all focus in one way or another upon Christ.

Jesus, like David, knew the wrath of the Father was something to fear, as He would have to endure it in His crucifixion. Jonathan Edwards (1703–1758) famously captured the nature of God's wrath in his famous sermon "Sinners in the Hands of an Angry God":

> O sinner! Consider the fearful danger you are in: 'tis a great furnace of wrath, a wide and bottomless pit, full of the fire of wrath, that you are

held over in the hand of that God, whose wrath
is provoked and incensed as much against you as
against many of the damned in hell; you hang by
a slender thread, with the flames of divine wrath
flashing about it, and ready every moment to singe
it, and burn it asunder; and you have no interest
in any mediator, and nothing to lay hold of to save
yourself, nothing to keep off the flames of wrath,
nothing of your own, nothing that you ever have
done, nothing that you can do, to induce God to
spare you one moment.[2]

While David knew that he justly merited God's wrath,
Jesus was perfectly sinless and in no way deserved it.
Rather, He willingly subjected Himself to His Father's
wrath so that Adam and Eve, Abraham, Isaac, Jacob,
David, and every other redeemed saint, including anyone
who takes shelter in God's mercy in Christ, would not
have to suffer His just wrath.

What comfort, peace, and joy to know, however, that
Christ took David's words upon His lips as He bore God's
wrath on our behalf so that we would not have to utter
them in hopelessness. Indeed, as Paul writes: "Therefore,
having been justified by faith, we have peace with God
through our Lord Jesus Christ" (Rom. 5:1). But this does
not mean we should consider our sin a light thing. Our
sin was not merely written off—far from it. The forgiveness of our sins was bought at a costly price: it cost God

---

2. Jonathan Edwards, "Sinners in the Hands of an Angry God," in
The Works of Jonathan Edwards (1834; repr., Edinburgh: Banner of Truth,
1992), 2:10.

His only begotten Son and it cost Jesus Christ His life, as He suffered an ignominious and painful death on the cross. In light of this truth, Paul tells the Corinthians:

> Flee sexual immorality. Every sin that a man does is outside the body, but he who commits sexual immorality sins against his own body. Or do you not know that your body is the temple of the Holy Spirit who is in you, whom you have from God, and you are not your own? For you were bought at a price; therefore glorify God in your body and in your spirit, which are God's. (1 Cor. 6:18–20)

We should therefore pray that the Lord through His Holy Spirit would make us acutely aware of our identity in Christ, our union with Him, and the incompatibility of sinful conduct with our identity.

Pray that you would not count sin a light matter but would instead realize the intensity of God's wrath, the costly sacrifice of Christ who bore that wrath for you, and then be led to repent of your sin and flee from it. However, even in the face of the consequence of our sin, we can still have joy, knowing that Christ has overcome our mortal enemy—death:

> "O Death, where is your sting?
> O Hades, where is your victory?"

> The sting of death is sin, and the strength of sin is the law. But thanks be to God, who gives us the victory through our Lord Jesus Christ. (1 Cor. 15:55–57)

We will not descend into the depths of death, where there is no remembrance of the Lord, where the dead do not praise Him. Rather, because of Christ, we will ascend to the heavens and join the great multitude of saints who stand before the throne of God and forever utter and sing the praises of the Lamb who was slain from the foundation of the world.

Conclusion

In the face of your sin, do not flee into darkness, but instead to the foot of the cross. When it seems as though you will never find God's favor because your sin is too great, find solace and comfort in the steadfast love of the Lord, which has been supremely revealed in Christ. Rejoice that Christ was greatly troubled in His soul so you do not have to carry that unbearable burden. And in the face of your sin, the prospects of God's just wrath, and even before your enemies, know that the Lord has heard your plea and will answer your prayer.

▶ **Questions for Further Study**

1. How are the prayers of Psalms 3–5 balanced by the prayer of Psalm 6 regarding the judgment of the wicked?

2. Is illness or persecution an automatic indicator that a Christian is guilty of hidden or secret sin?

3. What is the occasion of David's writing this psalm? What has he done?

4. David did not have to suffer God's wrath. How did Christ suffer it on his behalf?

▷ **Metrical Version of Psalm 6**

Pleading, 7.7.6.D.

No longer, Lord, despise me,
Nor in thy wrath chastise me,
Thy mercy I implore.
How long thine anger cherish?
Consumed thereby I perish;
My soul is troubled sore.

To me, O Lord, returning,
Save thou, with pity yearning.
Shall death thy mem'ry keep?
Or shall the grave confess thee?
Or I give thanks and bless thee,
While day and night I weep?

The Lord will ever hear me,
And when I pray be near me,
To put my foes to shame;
Turned back, no more to grieve me,
They suddenly shall leave me.
All glory to his Name!

—*Trinity Hymnal*, no. 511

CHAPTER 7

Song of Vindication

O LORD my God, if I have done this:
If there is iniquity in my hands,
If I have repaid evil to him who was at peace
    with me,
Or have plundered my enemy without cause,
Let the enemy pursue me and overtake me;
Yes, let him trample my life to the earth,
And lay my honor in the dust.

—PSALM 7:3–5

The seventh psalm is another personal lament, yet it is different from the previous ones we have explored because it responds to a false accusation. In Psalm 3, David's foes surrounded him. In Psalm 4, David's honor was somehow brought into question. In Psalm 5, David called upon the Lord to judge his enemies. In Psalm 6, David's cry was for the forgiveness of his sins. But in Psalm 7, David has been accused of wrongdoing, and he is innocent.

The title tells us that David was responding to the words of Cush, a Benjamite, but nothing in the biblical narrative informs us of this situation. Possibly the situation David writes about in Psalm 7 is similar to the time when Saul sought his life: "Then David fled from Naioth in Ramah, and went and said to Jonathan, "'What have I done? What is my iniquity, and what is my sin before your father, that he seeks my life?'" (1 Sam. 20:1). As we explore this psalm, we will see David's prayer for deliverance, his innocence, and God's righteousness and the fate of the wicked. But we must not forget that even though we are reading about false accusations against David, the Lord's anointed, we are also, in a sense, reading the thoughts of David's Greater Son, Jesus.

So often we read the Gospels and wonder what Jesus was thinking at certain points. What was He praying about when He secluded Himself from His disciples, for example? Psalms such as this one give us a window into Jesus' heart. Therefore, we must not immediately identify with David and think that he is uttering our thoughts when we are falsely accused of wrongdoing. Rather, we must first see this psalm as Christ's words. As Patrick Henry Reardon writes: "To pray this psalm properly is to enter into the mind of the Lord in the context of his redemptive Passion. It is not to give expression to our own personal feelings, but to discover something of his. It is to taste, in some measure, the bitterness and the gall."[1] In any account of a victim wronged, we more readily identify with the victim than the victimizer. For example, when we read about the prophet Hosea's pitiful marriage to his unfaithful wife, Gomer, we tend to align with Hosea. In Psalm 7, we are prone to place ourselves in David's shoes and see ourselves as the one falsely accused. Let's turn our

---

1. Patrick Henry Reardon, *Christ in the Psalms* (Ben Lomond, Calif.: Conciliar Press, 2000), 14.

reading of this psalm upside down and identify ourselves with the one who has falsely accused David.

David's Prayer for Deliverance

The psalm begins with David's cry to the Lord that He alone is the One in whom he takes refuge (v. 1). Recall what we have covered in previous chapters and bear in mind that the Psalter is not a random collection of reflections and thoughts. Rather, remember from Psalm 2 that David has acknowledged the One in whom people must seek refuge: the Messiah, the Anointed of the Lord, the King on God's holy hill, the Son of God. This is the overall context in which we must place David's cry. While David knows that the Son of God is his refuge, the intensity of the accusations against him is great. David describes them by using the metaphor of a lion tearing at its prey—ripping his soul to shreds (v. 2). While we do not know the specific nature of the accusations, we nevertheless should recognize they are vicious and false.

David's Innocence

David asserts his innocence in the face of these accusations. He does not claim to be completely righteous and free from all sin. Rather, his claim pertains to these specific false accusations. He is innocent—his hands are clean, and he is righteous *in this matter.* David's claims of innocence are so intense, he is willing to undergo God's judgment at the hands of his foes:

> If I have repaid evil to him who was at peace with me,
> Or have plundered my enemy without cause,

Let the enemy pursue me and overtake me;
Yes, let him trample my life to the earth,
And lay my honor in the dust. (vv. 4–5)

Our first thoughts might be that David's claims are strong
and perhaps unwarranted. After all, even if David is innocent, he still carries the guilt of other sins, doesn't he? We
must realize that David serves as a type, or foreshadow, of
Christ, and, as such, his innocence points forward to the
perfect innocence and righteousness of Jesus, something
we will see in greater detail. Nevertheless, David's claims
should not unsettle us, but rather give us hope because we
have the blessing of resting in the perfect righteousness of
Jesus. This was ultimately the ground of David's hope and
the reason he was willing to enter the tribunal of the Lord
and ask for a verdict in his favor.

God's Righteousness and the Fate of the Wicked

From this context David calls the Lord to take His seat
in the great cosmic courtroom—to assume the throne of
judgment in verses 6–8:

Arise, O LORD, in Your anger;
Lift Yourself up because of the rage of my enemies;
Rise up for me to the judgment You have commanded!
So the congregation of the peoples shall surround You;
For their sakes, therefore, return on high.
The LORD shall judge the peoples;
Judge me, O LORD, according to my righteousness,
And according to my integrity within me.

This is an ominous setting, a courtroom like no other,
as the Judge is no mere human being who can be swayed

by persuasive reasoning to embrace a shoddy argument, bribed with money under the table, or biased with clouded judgment. On the contrary, David tells us at the end of verse 9 that God is a righteous judge—He judges according to the truth, nothing less than His holy and moral character. Moreover, not only is God a holy and righteous judge but He is also perfect in His verdicts because, as we read in verse 9, He "tests the hearts and minds."

God does not judge based on external appearances; He knows the depths of man's heart. He gazes into man's heart and lays bare every thought, intention, and inclination. Thus, there is no hiding from His all-seeing, omniscient eyes. We might expect David to call for the judgment of his enemies who have falsely accused him of wrongdoing. Yet he is open to the possibility that his accusers might repent of their sin, in which case we can assume that David would forgive them. So while David prays for judgment against the wicked, like in Psalms 3 through 5, his request is balanced by his acute awareness of his own sin (the subject of Psalm 6) and his willingness to forgive those who have sinned against him.

However, in verses 12 and 13, David calls for God's judgment to fall upon those who do not repent:

> If he does not turn back,
> He will sharpen His sword;
> He bends His bow and makes it ready.
> He also prepares for Himself instruments of death;
> He makes His arrows into fiery shafts.

David uses the powerful imagery of God sharpening His sword, drawing back His bow, and lighting arrows with fire—all to be used against the unrepentant man. Because this sinful accuser is unrepentant, David writes in verses 14–16 that the sinner has brought this judgment upon himself. A person who stands before the Judge of the cosmos and knowingly lies, trying to deceive an all-knowing and all-seeing God, is wasting time on an exercise in futility.

Such an act comes crashing back upon the unrepentant sinner's face. In verse 15, David describes such a person as one who has dug his own hole and fallen into it; also, his deception violently collides with his own skull. In this psalm we ultimately do not know the outcome of this trial before the Creator of the cosmos because David does not reveal the final verdict. However, we do know David's attitude and the hope he places in the Lord as he awaits the vindicatory verdict: "I will praise the LORD according to His righteousness, and will sing praise to the name of the LORD Most High" (v. 17). David's confidence resides not in himself, but in the Lord. Innocent people can often be filled with great trepidation as they enter a courtroom because even though they know they are innocent, others might not see it their way. However, before God's throne, there is no chance of a miscarriage of justice, so David sings with confidence knowing that the Lord will judge righteously and ultimately vindicate him.

The Messiah's Suffering

Again, the place to start as we reflect upon David's psalm is with Christ. Usually we are ready to identify with the one suffering persecution rather than the one who inflicts it. We must not forget that David prefigures Jesus; the messiah points to the Messiah, David's Greater Son. We know that Jesus was falsely accused of grievous sin. David's claim to righteousness was merely in relation to these false accusations; he could not claim perfect sinlessness, let alone perfect fulfillment of the law.

Jesus, his Greater Son, was perfectly sinless and completely, down to the last jot and tittle, fulfilled the whole law. Yet in spite of Christ's perfect obedience, He experienced the following:

- He was accused of blasphemy (Matt. 26:65; Mark 14:64; John 10:33).

- He constantly fought off verbal assaults and attacks (John 8:39).

- He was betrayed by one of His disciples for thirty pieces of silver (Zech. 11:12–13; Matt. 26:15; 27:9).

- He prayed in the garden and hoped that His closest personal friends would vigilantly pray with Him, only to find that they had fallen asleep in His darkest hour (Luke 22:40–46).

- He was denied three times by one of His closest friends and disciples (Matt. 26:34, 74–75; Mark 14:30, 72; Luke 22:34, 60–61; John 13:38; 18:27).

- He was unjustly and cruelly beaten by those who were supposed to uphold righteousness (John 19:3).

- He was betrayed by His countrymen when they had the opportunity to free Him; instead they chose a common criminal who was guilty of murder (Matt. 27:16–26).

- He was mocked by those who falsely accused Him as He hung naked upon the cross (Mark 15:35–36).

In all of this, Jesus' false accusers tore Him apart like a lion ripping pieces of flesh from its prey.

To whom did Christ entrust His life? To whom did Jesus cry out not only before His crucifixion but also during His intense suffering? He cried out to His God and Father and committed Himself into the hands of the perfect and righteous Judge. In David's case, we do not know the outcome, but in Jesus' case, we do. God overturned the unjust and false verdict that His Son was guilty and declared that He was righteous by raising Him from the dead. Paul writes:

> And without controversy great is the mystery of godliness:
>
>> God was manifested in the flesh,
>> Justified in the Spirit,
>> Seen by angels,
>> Preached among the Gentiles,
>> Believed on in the world,
>> Received up in glory. (1 Tim. 3:16)

What we must realize is that Christ bore the penalty for our sin when He suffered throughout His life and on the cross.

If we approach this psalm, then, through the crucified Christ, we must first realize that we are the reason Christ suffered on the cross—for our sins, our false accusations, and our rebellion against Him. Apart from God's grace in Christ, we too would have been chanting with the crowds, "Give us Barabbas! We have no king but Caesar!" Therefore, we must always ask the Lord to help us see our own sin before we think of ourselves as better than others and adopt the role of the martyr.

Moreover, remember that for us to step into the cosmic courtroom and ask God to judge us is not the same as going before a judge in an earthly court who will see only external appearances: "All the churches shall know that I am He who searches the minds and hearts. And I will give to each one of you according to your works" (Rev. 2:23). To ask God to judge us according to our works is to invite certain doom and judgment upon our heads. However, if we follow David, who sought shelter in the Lord's Anointed, Jesus Christ, then the Lord sees Christ's righteousness rather than our sinfulness. Moreover, when we find ourselves in situations in which we have been unjustly or falsely accused of wrong, we will hopefully see these accusations in two principal ways.

First, we will see these things not as random happenings, but as part of the sufferings of Christ. Notice how Jesus characterized Saul's persecution of the church: "Saul, Saul, why are you persecuting *Me*?" (Acts 9:4, emphasis added). Saul persecuted the church, but Jesus accused him of persecuting Him. To persecute the church is to persecute Jesus; to persecute the body is to persecute the Head. Just as unbelievers persecuted Christ, our Head, so will they persecute His body, the church: "Remember the word that I said to you, 'A servant is not greater than his master.' If they persecuted Me, they will also persecute you" (John 15:20).

Second, in light of our union with Christ, when we do encounter false accusations, we should approach such situations in a Christlike manner. This means that we will look humbly, patiently, and mercifully upon those who make such false claims against us because we will remember the mercy, grace, and love that God has shown us, we who were pregnant with mischief and gave birth to lies (v. 14). We will then face such false accusations with the hope that the Lord will have mercy upon our foes and cause them to repent, and we will rejoice when they do!

However, in our response to those who refuse to repent, we can and must sing with David: "I will praise the LORD according to His righteousness, and will sing praise to the name of the LORD most high" (v. 17). We will sing these words because we know that God will, on the last day, right all wrongs when Christ returns to judge the world. Also, when we find ourselves in such situations, we should examine our hearts and seriously ask whether we have falsely accused anyone. So often in our intense scrutiny of others' peccadilloes we fail to see our own grievous sins. We need to remember that this self-examination of our motives and intentions must pass the test of God's scrutiny, as He is the One who sees and knows everything. This is what Paul and the apostles did: "For our exhortation did not come from error or uncleanness, nor was it in deceit. But as we have been approved by God to be entrusted with the gospel, even so we speak, not as pleasing men, but God who tests our hearts" (1 Thess. 2:3–4).

Conclusion

This psalm presents another dimension of the Christian life as we await the return of the enthroned Messiah of Psalm 2. Given the global messianic conflict between the wicked and those who have sought shelter in Christ, the Anointed, we know that we will be falsely accused of wrongdoing as David and Christ were. Nevertheless, as we reflect on this psalm, let us not do so with an eye to our own meager sufferings, the relatively minor false accusations that we suffer. In doing so, we risk mounting our high horse of pride and arrogance. Rather, let us look at this psalm through the lens of the crucified Christ. Pray this psalm, and enter into the mind of the Lord in the context of His suffering and crucifixion. We must not be quick to run to our feelings but instead plumb the depths of Christ's sufferings—to taste only a fraction of the bitterness of the gall. And in so doing, the gaze of our faith falls upon the crucified and risen Messiah, and we know that we have received the forgiveness of sins and His righteousness. Gaze upon Christ, knowing that He will, in the end, right all wrongs.

▶ **Questions for Further Study**

1. How could David claim to be innocent?

2. In whom had David taken shelter?

3. How long might those who have entrusted their reputations to the Lord have to wait before they are finally and completely vindicated from false charges?

4. When we apply this psalm, how should we view ourselves so that we see Christ in it? Do we begin with Him or with us?

▷ Metrical Version of Psalm 7
Dalehurst, C.M.

O Lord my God, in thee do I my confidence repose:
Save and deliver me from all my persecuting foes;

Lest that the enemy my soul should, like a lion tear,
In pieces rending it, while there is no deliverer.

O Lord my God, if it be so that I committed this;
If it be so that in my hands iniquity there is:

If I rewarded ill to him that was at peace with me;
(Yea, ev'n the man that without cause my foe was
   I did free;)

Then let the foe pursue and take my soul, and my
   life thrust
Down to the earth, and let him lay mine honour
   in the dust.

Rise in thy wrath, Lord, raise thyself, for my foes
   raging be;
And, to the judgment which thou hast commanded,
   wake for me.

So shall th' assembly of thy folk about encompass thee:
Thou, therefore, for their sakes, return unto thy place
   on high.

The Lord he shall the people judge: my judge,
   Jehovah, be.
After my righteousness, and mine integrity in me.

O let the wicked's malice end; but stablish stedfastly
The righteous: for the righteous God the hearts and
   reins doth try.

In God, who saves th' upright in heart, is my defense
   and stay.
God just men judgeth, God is wroth with ill men
   ev'ry day.

If he do not return again, then he his sword will whet;
His bow he hath already bent, and hath it ready set:

He also hath for him prepar'd the instruments of death;
Against the persecutors he his shafts ordained hath.

Behold, he with iniquity doth travail, as in birth;
A mischief he conceived hath, and falsehood shall
   bring forth.

He made a pit and digg'd it deep, another there to take;
But he is fall'n into the ditch which he himself did make.

Upon his own head his mischief shall be returned home;
His vi'lent dealing also down on his own pate shall come.

According to his righteousness the Lord I'll magnify;
And will sing praise unto the name of God that is
   most high.

           —1650 *Scottish Psalter* as it appears in *The Psalms of*
           David in Metre: According to the Version Approved
           by The Church of Scotland, 5–6

CHAPTER 8

Song of Majesty

When I consider Your heavens, the work of Your fingers,
The moon and the stars, which You have ordained,
What is man that You are mindful of him,
And the son of man that You visit him?
For You have made him a little lower than the angels,
And You have crowned him with glory and honor.
—PSALM 8:3–5

From the beginning of our survey of Psalms 1–8, we have seen two key motifs develop. First, the righteous man of Psalm 1 is none other than Jesus Christ, the One who never walked in the counsel of the wicked or sat in the seat of scorners. Rather, throughout the entirety of Jesus' earthly ministry, His delight was in the law of the Lord, and He meditated on it day and night. The psalmist tells us that this righteous man, Jesus, was also the Anointed One, the Messiah, the One whom God has installed as King upon His holy hill.

Second, this righteous man is not unopposed. The wicked are like the chaff that the wind drives away, and they are the ones who rage against the Lord and His Anointed. They are the ones who think they can throw off the authority of the Lord and His Messiah. The subsequent psalms then present a pitched battle between the righteous and the wicked—between David, the Lord's messiah, and those who persecute him. What these psalms say about David is ultimately what they are saying of his Greater Son, Jesus. We begin on a mountaintop, with the revelation of the righteous man and His coming reign as Messiah, only to plunge into the depths of persecution, darkness, and despair.

David's initial anointing as the future king of Israel was undoubtedly personally and emotionally exhilarating for the young shepherd, but his enthusiasm and faith were undoubtedly challenged as he descended from that peak into the valley of darkness. He went from being identified and anointed as king to eventually running for his life— he had to flee from the wicked king. Nevertheless, just as David's flight ended with his ascent out of the darkness to the king's throne, in Psalm 8 we have something of an ascent from the darkness of persecution and trials in some of the previous psalms.

In many respects, these first eight chapters set the tone for the rest of the first book of the Psalter, and even the whole book, in that they begin in joy and jubilation, descend into darkness and trial, and reemerge into joy and jubilation. In the eighth psalm David writes a song of praise in which he not only extols God as creator but also rejoices in the blessings that He has poured out on man. However, David does not merely have the creation of man in view here, however praiseworthy it is. Rather, he ultimately offers a hymn of praise for the true Son of Man, Jesus Christ. Let us see how this psalm is a hymn of praise to Christ our Lord and how we too should be filled with joy, praise, and thanksgiving for the reign of Jesus the Messiah. We can ascend out of the darkness, persecution, and suffering of Psalms 3–7 and emerge into the hope of the consummated reign of the enthroned Messiah.

Intimate Praise

The psalm begins with what are perhaps some of the most familiar words from the Psalter:

> O LORD our Lord,
> How excellent is Your name in all the earth,
> Who have set Your glory above the heavens! (v. 1)

We see right away that David's words of praise reveal the intimate nature of his relationship with the God He praises. He begins the psalm with the covenant name of God—Yahweh—which is typically translated into LORD, using all capital letters. We should keep in mind that God first revealed His covenant name to Moses and His people out of the burning bush on Mount Horeb (Ex. 3:1–15).

This is no mere personal introduction, like two people exchanging names at a cocktail party. Rather, we associate calling someone by his or her first name with intimacy and familiarity. Perhaps in our day this is something that has been lost, as people are all too comfortable not only with calling someone by his first name but perhaps by something even less, such as "Dude," or "Hey you!" Nevertheless, it is often considered impolite to call a person by his first name unless we have been given explicit permission to do so. This etiquette rule only hints of the intimacy and privilege associated with calling God by His covenant name. To call God Yahweh means to be in covenant with Him—to know Him as He has chosen to reveal Himself to His people.

However, David follows God's covenant name with a title, Adonai, rendered in English as *Lord*, using lowercase letters. An *adonai* is one who rules or governs, so this combination of the covenant name of God with the title tells us that God rules over all of creation. "Oh Yahweh, our *Adonai*, how majestic is Your name in all the earth!" It is not just that David's praise fills his heart but the entire creation breaks forth in praise of its Creator. David tells us that babes and infants sing forth the praise of God, and not even God's enemies can suppress His rule (v. 2). In other words, the battle reflected in Psalms 3–7 has been fierce, but the wicked will not suppress the rule of God and His Anointed.

Praise for the Creation

As David reflects on Yahweh's rule over the creation, he casts his eye on it and, in particular, the creation of man. He casts his gaze upon the creation of the heavens and marvels at the beauty he sees—he admires the moon and stars, all of which God has created (v. 3). Against this backdrop of grandeur and beauty, David looks upon man and wonders: "What is man that You are mindful of him, and the son of man that You visit him?" (v. 4). It is easy to grasp something of David's wonderment.

Consider the vastness of the cosmos, how it stretches for billions and billions of light years, yet in all the immensity of this grand and marvelous universe, God has chosen to be mindful of a seemingly insignificant creature, man. Out of this vast and expansive creation, why has God cast

His care on man? In spite of man's relative insignificance against the backdrop of the vast cosmos, David points out that God has invested man with special privileges: "For You have made him a little lower than the angels, and You have crowned him with glory and honor" (v. 5). In what way has God crowned man?

Not only has God given man honor and glory, but, as the following verses intimate, He has also given him dominion over the works of His hands and put all things under his feet. To be under someone's feet means to be under his authority. This leads David to reflect on the creation of man in the temple-garden of Eden and the Genesis dominion mandate (Gen. 1:28). As David considers man's creation, he recalls how Yahweh, as the King of the cosmos, placed all of the creation under Adam's rule—all sheep and oxen, the beasts of the field, birds of the heavens, and the fish of the sea—indeed, all the creation! The thought of God's investiture of man with glory, honor, and the position of authority causes David to break forth into praise once again and end the psalm as he began it: "O LORD our Lord, how excellent is Your name in all the earth!" (v. 9).

David has risen out of the depths of despair and has ascended the heights of joy, praise, and thanksgiving. However, some people who read this psalm feel a gnawing sense of unease. We can rejoice with David at the wonderful blessings God has poured out upon man. But as we read, we may do so with a sense of loss and mourning. We know all too well that Adam fell from these glorious heights into sin and rebellion and forfeited his dominion over the creation. Adam opened the floodgates of iniquity and started the greatest conflict in the history of the earth, the battle between the wicked and the Lord's Anointed. Therefore, can we join with David and sing the praises of God regarding the wonderful blessings He has poured out on man in his creation if he has squandered and spit on the gifts he has received?

Praise for the Son of Man

How can David sing the praises of God, knowing well the sinfulness of man, which is evident in Psalms 1–7? The answer comes once again from Christ, and I use the title *Christ*, rather than the name *Jesus*, for a specific reason. The title *Christ* indicates the Messiah, the Anointed. The Psalter begins, you recall, with the righteous man, the Christ who ascends Mount Zion, God's holy hill, to rule over the rebellious nations. The Messiah would restore God's reign over the creation—He would subdue God's enemies. We see this picture in Daniel 7, which describes one of the prophet's famous visions. Four ferocious beasts arise out of the waters and roam the earth, killing and destroying. Daniel specifically tells us that these beasts had dominion. In Daniel's vision, the creation is upside down! The creatures have dominion, not man.

But when God comes on His fiery chariot, He takes away their dominion and gives it to one like the Son of Man, one like Adam, who comes riding on the clouds and gives Him an everlasting dominion and kingdom. A Son of Man, one like Adam, would restore God's rule throughout the creation, and we know that this one like Adam was the Anointed, the Messiah. We find ample confirmation of this in the New Testament, as many passages join in the chorus of praise, identifying Jesus as the Son of Man. When Jesus rode into Jerusalem on the foal of a colt, the children cried out: "Hosanna to the Son of David!" (Matt. 21:15).

First, do not overlook the children's identification of Jesus as David's Greater Son. The children of Jerusalem recognized Jesus as the one of whom David wrote. When the Pharisees became indignant and tried to rebuke Jesus for allowing the children to say such a thing, how did He respond? Matthew records Jesus' words: "Have you never read, 'Out of the mouth of babes and nursing infants You have perfected praise'?" (21:16). Jesus quotes Psalm 8 and, in effect, tells the Pharisees, "The children are correct! Don't you know that David wrote Psalm 8 about Me?"

Jesus, of course, was not alone in making the connection between Psalm 8 and Him. The author of Hebrews gives us an infallible, inerrant, and authoritative interpretation and commentary upon Psalm 8:

> But one testified in a certain place, saying:
>
> "What is man that You are mindful of him,
> Or the son of man that You take care of him?
> You have made him a little lower than the angels;
> You have crowned him with glory and honor,
> And set him over the works of Your hands.
> You have put all things in subjection under his feet."
>
> For in that He put all in subjection under him, He left nothing that is not put under him. But now we do not yet see all things put under him. But we see Jesus, who was made a little lower than the angels, for the suffering of death crowned with

> glory and honor, that He, by the grace of God,
> might taste death for everyone. (2:6–9)

David writes ultimately about the Messiah, Jesus, and the author of Hebrews confirms this. Moreover, Christ not only ascended Mount Zion, God's holy hill, to restore God's rule over the creation, but He also suffered and died so that sinful man might once again regain the place of honor and glory that he once had.

In other words, Christ is not only the King of kings but He is also the sacrifice that brings the forgiveness of sins, enabling those who seek shelter in Him to regain a far better place than Adam ever had. Jesus does not merely return us to the garden where we are left to our own devices and where we might fall into sin and rebellion once again. No—Jesus brings us to an indefectible state. He permanently and irreversibly brings us into the new creation, the new heaven and earth, where He, as the true, obedient, and faithful Son of Man, rules. Like the author of Hebrews, the apostle Paul embraces these themes and echoes Psalm 8 in his letter to the Ephesians:

> And what is the exceeding greatness of His power toward us who believe, according to the working of His mighty power which He worked in Christ when He raised Him from the dead and seated Him at His right hand in the heavenly places, far above all principality and power and might and dominion, and every name that is named, not only in this age but also in that which is to come.
>
> And He put all things under His feet, and gave Him to be head over all things to the church,

which is His body, the fullness of Him who fills
all in all. (1:19–23)

Those who are united to Christ by faith through the
indwelling power and presence of the Holy Spirit are once
again crowned with glory and honor and rule over the
creation with the last Adam, the Messiah, the Christ.

However, there is even greater reason to rejoice
because not only will Jesus as the Son of Man restore
God's rule over the creation but He will also subdue
all His enemies—all those whom Daniel characterizes
as beasts—including the chief enemy, death itself. Paul
invokes Psalm 8 again in his explanation of the signifi-
cance of the resurrection of the Christ of Psalm 2: "For
He must reign till He has put all enemies under His feet.
The last enemy that will be destroyed is death. For 'He
has put all things under His feet.' But when He says 'all
things are put under Him,' it is evident that He who put
all things under Him is excepted" (1 Cor. 15:25–27).

The prospects of the future reign of David's Greater
Son, Jesus the Messiah, filled him with praise. Yes, David
looked back upon man and his creation and reflected
upon the glory, honor, and authority God had given to
him. But even in the face of man's ignominious fall into
rebellion and forfeiture of his God-given reign over the
creation to Satan, sin, and death, it was the prospect of
the future reign of the Son of Man, David's Greater Son,
that filled him with praise, joy, and thanksgiving for his
great and marvelous covenant Lord. David knew that his
persecution, trials, and the seemingly unchecked conduct
of the wicked of Psalms 3–5 would come to an end, one

that would culminate in the reign of man over the creation once again, but this time it would be the reign of the Messiah, the Son of Man, Jesus.

This brings the weightiest of consequences for understanding not only the Psalms but ultimately the Old Testament. When we read Psalm 8, we are ultimately reading a prophecy of the coming reign of Jesus. If you doubt this conclusion, you should reread Hebrews 2, Ephesians 1, and 1 Corinthians 15 or meditate on the fact that Jesus' favorite title for Himself was Son of Man, which comes from, among other passages, Psalm 8. But we must press the point even further—back to the very beginning. If Psalm 8 is a prophecy of Christ, then we must realize that the opening chapter of the Bible serves the same purpose.

Jesus the Messiah is no mere afterthought, something tacked onto a well-intended but nevertheless disastrous first attempt—something cobbled together on the heels of Adam's unthinkable and unforeseen rebellion. Far from it! Rather, God had the reign and kingdom of Jesus Christ in mind long before He first reached down into the dust of the earth and formed man and breathed life into him (Gen. 2:7). Christ, therefore, defines who man is supposed to be—Christ is the true man. Genesis 1 and Psalm 8 are prophecies of the universal subjection of the creation to the reign of Jesus the Christ. Genesis 1 and Psalm 8, therefore, are not primarily about man—museum relics of a lost and fallen kingdom covered by the sands of time—but rather prophetic promises of Jesus' reign, one that has been inaugurated in His resurrection and ascension and will culminate in His conquest of Satan, sin, and death when He hands the kingdom over to His Father.

Conclusion

As we look out upon the creation, it seems as though the beasts have dominion rather than man. Or, in other words, reflect upon David's cries for God's assistance and grace in Psalms 3–7 and then cast your gaze upon Christ as He is seated in the heavenly places—and remember that you are seated there with Him. Rejoice with King David and cry out with joy, thanksgiving, and praise: Yahweh, our Lord, how majestic is Your name in all the earth! How majestic is the name of Jesus the Christ in all the earth!

▶ **Questions for Further Study**

1. How does Psalm 8 relate to the previous psalms?

2. In what way is Psalm 8 prophetic of Christ's reign?

3. Identify a passage in the New Testament that applies Psalm 8 to the ministry and especially the resurrection of Christ.

4. To what hope did David ultimately cling in the midst of his suffering?

5. How is Genesis 1 prophetic of Christ's ministry? Read Romans 5:14 for a hint.

▶ Metrical Version of Psalm 8

Dundee, C. M.

How excellent in all the earth, Lord, our Lord,
     is thy name!
Who hast thy glory far advanc'd above the
     starry frame.

From infants' and from sucklings' mouth thou
     didest strength ordain,
For thy foes cause, that so thou might'st th'
     avenging foe restrain.

When I look up unto the heav'ns, which thine
     own fingers fram'd,
Unto the moon, and to the stars, which were by
     thee ordained;

Then say I, What is man, that he remember'd is
     by thee?
Or what the son of man, that thou so kind to him
     should'st be?

For thou a little lower hast him than the
     angels made;
With glory and with dignity thou crowned hast
     his head.

Of thy hands' works thou mad'st him lord, all
     under's feet didst lay;
All sheep and oxen, yea, and beasts that in the
     field do stray;

Fowls of the air, fish of the sea, all that pass
    through the same.
How excellent in all the earth, Lord, our Lord,
    is thy name!

—1650 *Scottish Psalter* as it appears in
*The Psalms of David in Metre: According
to the Version Approved by The
Church of Scotland*, 6–7

Conclusion

The Psalms are a beautiful ode to the person and work of Christ, and I hope that through this small survey of the first eight psalms you have a greater appreciation for the structure, organization, and especially the substance of them: Jesus Christ. When we read the Psalms, or any passage of Scripture for that matter, we should first ask in what way Christ is organically and legitimately present in the text. The numerous quotations of and allusions to Psalms 1–8 in the New Testament reveal that the apostles believed that the Psalms principally spoke of Christ. This is especially evident because of the numerous times that Psalm 8 appears in the New Testament. The apostles knew that Psalm 8 was a reflection about the creation of man, but they also recognized that it was a prophecy of Christ's reign. Once we rightly recognize where Christ appears in the Psalms, we have the proper footing from which to understand our own connection to them. When we read, for example, of the righteous man of Psalm 1 and recognize that Christ is that man, then through our union with Christ we have the hope of reflecting His righteousness.

Another important benefit of studying and knowing the Psalms is that we are equipped for difficult circumstances in life. Second Timothy 3:16–17 tells us that all Scripture is "given by inspiration of God, and is profitable for doctrine, for reproof, for correction, for instruction in righteousness," so that believers would be "thoroughly equipped for every good work." But there are many churches for whom large portions of the Bible are a mystery because they never surface in preaching, liturgy, or worship. The Psalms, for example, encompass a wide variety of genres, one of which is the personal lament, such as Psalms 3–7. Often we hear of praise music and the praise team, but we never hear of a lament team. In other words, too many churches try to make worship fun, exciting, and joyful, which from one vantage point is understandable. But many people in the church suffer, lack joy, and feel as though they are out of place because of how they feel. But if churches regularly included personal laments from the Psalms in their worship, whether in preaching or congregational singing, it would signal to those who suffer that they too have a place in the church. To put it in more popular terms, the church can be a place where you go to sing the blues.

The Psalms encompass every dimension of life—joy, praise, lament, anger, and repentance—which makes them eminently important for the spiritual well-being of the church. With a Christ-centered approach to the Psalms, we can rejoice in the victory that we have through Christ, such as in Psalm 2, but when we feel oppressed, afflicted, or even persecuted, we can flee to Christ in Psalms 3–7, knowing that the darkness will give way to the light of Psalm 8 and the glorious consummation of all things. I hope that through this survey of the first eight psalms of the Psalter you have had a taste of the manna from heaven and that you will hunger all the more so you will explore the rest of the book of Psalms. Whether in plenty or want, in joy or sorrow, read, meditate, pray, and by all means sing to Christ and cry out with the psalmist, "O LORD our Lord, how excellent is Your name in all the earth!"